MILESTONES
IN MODERN
WORLD HISTORY

The Bolshevik
Revolution

MILESTONES
IN MODERN
WORLD HISTORY

The Bolshevik Revolution

The Chinese Cultural
Revolution

The Collapse of
the Soviet Union

D-Day and the Liberation
of France

The End of Apartheid
in South Africa

The Iranian Revolution

The Treaty of Versailles

The Universal Declaration
of Human Rights

The Bolshevik Revolution

JOHN C. DAVENPORT

CHELSEA HOUSE
PUBLISHERS
An imprint of Infobase Publishing

The Bolshevik Revolution

Chelsea House
An imprint of Infobase Publishing
132 West 31st Street
New York, NY 10001

Library of Congress Cataloging-in-Publication Data

Davenport, John, 1960–
  The Bolshevik Revolution / John C. Davenport.
    p. cm. — (Milestones in modern world history)
  Includes bibliographical references and index.
  ISBN 978-1-60413-279-3 (hardcover : alk. paper) 1. Soviet Union—History—Revolution, 1917–1921—Juvenile literature. 2. Russia—History—1801–1917—Juvenile literature. I. Title. II. Series.

  DK265.D297 2009
  947.084'1—dc22   2008054807

Chelsea House books are available at special discounts when purchased in bulk quantities for businesses, associations, institutions, or sales promotions. Please call our Special Sales Department in New York at (212) 967-8800 or (800) 322-8755.

You can find Chelsea House on the World Wide Web at http://www.chelseahouse.com.

Text design by Erik Lindstrom
Cover design by Alicia Post
Composition by Facts On File, New York, NY
Cover printed by Yurchak Printing, Landisville, Pa.
Book printed and bound by Yurchak Printing, Landisville, Pa.
Printed in the United States of America

This book is printed on acid-free paper.

All links and Web addresses were checked and verified to be correct at the time of publication. Because of the dynamic nature of the Web, some addresses and links may have changed since publication and may no longer be valid.

CONTENTS

Killing the Tsar

Nicholas II, Tsar of All the Russias, last of the mighty Romanovs, waited for a decision from his captors—life or death. For nearly three months, he and his family had languished as prisoners, first in the Russian capital of Petrograd, once called St. Petersburg, and then in a small house near the Ural city of Yekaterinburg. Ever since he had willingly given up the Russian throne in March 1917, Nicholas II had been forced to suffer one indignity after another at the hands of his political opponents. Now he sat under arrest, far from both the center of power and the swirling events of the revolution that had brought him down.

But at least he had his family. What would have been a miserable and lonely imprisonment was brightened somewhat by the presence of those the tsar loved. Nicholas II had with him his beautiful and devoted wife, Alexandra, who had long been a consolation to him during the dark days of upheaval that had begun just as the tide of World War I (1914-1918) had turned against Russia in favor of its German enemy. Alexandra brought a few rays of joyful light into her husband's bleak life. Similarly, Nicholas's son, Alexei, lit up the tsar's otherwise miserable existence. The boy loved his father deeply and cherished each moment they spent together. Nicholas, for his part, doted on Alexei. The fact that the 13-year-old heir to the royal throne suffered from hemophilia, an incurable blood disease, only amplified the love his father felt for him. Rounding out the tsar's family entourage were his four daughters: Olga, Tatiana, Maria, and the irrepressible Anastasia. Extroverted and tomboyish, Anastasia occupied a special place in Nicholas's heart.

Sharing the Romanov family's captivity were the family doctor, Alexandra's maid, Nicholas's valet, and the imperial couple's private cook. In all, 11 members of the royal household languished in the Ipatiev House in Yekaterinburg as prisoners of men who were determined to bring Russia into a new world in which royal families and absolute monarchs had no place. The Romanovs' captors envisioned a Russia without autocracy, without tsars. These revolutionary men were called Bolsheviks. They sought to empower the common people and inaugurate a working-class dictatorship that would remove capitalism from Russia and eventually from the world. This historic mission could not be successfully accomplished while Nicholas and his line of future rulers existed.

Near midnight on July 16, 1918, orders arrived in Yekaterinburg to terminate that line. The commander of the unit guarding the Romanovs, Yakov Yurovsky, brought his men together and pronounced the tsar's death sentence. "We must shoot them all tonight," Yurovsky said dryly.[1] The Bolshevik leadership no longer had any practical use for the royal family; in fact, they had become a distinct liability. Earlier in their revolution, the Bolsheviks had hoped to use the Romanovs as

The last tsar of Russia, Nicholas II, with his wife, Tsarina Alexandra, and their children, from left to right: Princess Olga, Princess Maria, Princess Anastasia, Prince Alexei and Princess Tatiana. An absolute monarch, Nicholas ruled from 1894 until his abdication in March 1917.

bargaining chips in their negotiations with the revolutionary government's political opponents. Since the Bolshevik seizure of power in October 1917, men steadfastly loyal to the tsar had fought to place him back on the throne. They had taken up arms and launched themselves into a civil war against the

Bolshevik regime. Elements of their White Army, as opposed to the Bolshevik Red Army, now were approaching Yekaterinburg. The Romanov family, far from being a useful tool, had become a genuine threat. If the advancing Whites liberated the tsar and his family, Nicholas II would become a counterrevolutionary icon, a rallying point for the anti-Bolshevik coalition. The Bolsheviks could not allow this to happen. Nicholas and everyone related to him had to die, now.

Thus, in the late-night hours of July 16, the guards awakened the royals. Nicholas and his entourage were roused from their beds and told to prepare to be moved. The soldiers told the imperial family that there was "trouble in the city, and [they] would have to take them to another, safer place."[2] The family washed and dressed hurriedly and were denied any imperial finery; Nicholas and his young son were compelled to pull on simple tunics and caps of the type worn by common soldiers. Alexandra and her daughters slipped into plain dresses, but those worn by Maria and Anastasia had sewn within them a secret cache of smuggled imperial jewels. The two girls had stitched the gems into their dresses for safekeeping, fully expecting to wear them proudly again someday.

After bathing and dressing, the Romanovs, at 1:00 A.M. on July 17, were led to the basement of the Ipatiev House. There they found the cellar empty except for three chairs set up in the middle of the room. The guards directed the tsar, his wife, and their son toward these. The rest of the party filed in behind and around the royal couple. When one of the doomed captives commented on the chairs and how everyone was being pushed together, a soldier replied that the family was being posed for an official photograph. The children sensed no imminent danger, and their elders felt a sense of relief that the long ordeal of captivity might soon be over. One of the Bolshevik troops, indeed, later recalled how "none of the Tsar's family asked any questions. They did not weep or cry."[3] Another commented that the "Romanovs were completely calm, no suspicions."[4]

The tension finally broke when Yurovsky and 11 officers entered the room, one executioner for each of the prisoners. Yurovsky had assigned the men to specific members of the royal family "so that [they] would not suffer and have to witness each other's deaths."[5] As he entered the room, Nicholas and Alexandra stood up, sensing instinctively that some sort of important announcement was about to be made. "In view of the fact that your relatives are continuing their attack on Soviet Russia," Yurovsky read out, "the Ural Executive Committee has decided to execute you."[6] Nicholas, in disbelief, staggered backward and screamed, "Oh, my God! . . . Oh, my God! No!" His wife and daughters frantically crossed themselves. "What? What?" the tsar exclaimed.[7] "This!" Yurovsky responded.[8] With that, the executioners raised their weapons and fired. Tsar Nicholas II died instantly, shot through the head at close range. His wife was similarly killed outright as the executioners began pouring bullets into the imperial victims. Olga, the eldest royal daughter, fell next as a round smashed into her skull. The family physician, Nicholas's valet, and the imperial cook collapsed next to her. As the shooting intensified, bullets flying about the room, the young Prince Alexei lunged toward his father's slumped corpse and grabbed onto one of the dead tsar's blood-soaked legs. His killers rushed forward and kicked the tsarevich to the ground. One of them then put his rifle to the boy's ear and shot twice. The rounds fired at Maria and Anastasia hit their mark, but they ricocheted off of the jewels that both girls had secreted away in the stitching of their dresses. Desperately struggling to live, the princesses fell to the floor and covered their heads with their arms. It proved to be a hopeless effort; each was shot repeatedly in the head and neck. Alexandra's maid was denied the quick end of a bullet; she was stabbed to death with a bayonet.

For 20 long minutes, the killing squad allowed the bodies of the Romanov family to lie undisturbed in a spreading pool of blood. Only then did they move forward to check the bod-

Pictured, the room in Yekaterinburg, Siberia, Russia where Nicholas II and the other members of the Romanov family were executed on July 17, 1918.

ies for any lingering signs of life. The soldiers turned over one body, then another, checking for pulses. Suddenly, one of the tsar's daughters screamed in pain. Having survived the bullets, she was set upon by several men who bayoneted her dozens of times and crushed her skull with blows from their rifle butts. The last of the Romanovs was dead. Russia would never again bow down before a tsar.

The corpses were dragged from the crimson-stained basement at 6:00 A.M. Taken to a nearby forest, the bodies were met by 25 conscripted workers sent to help dispose of the royal remains. The bodies were promptly laid out in a neat line. The workers stripped each one and searched both the corpses and the clothing for hidden valuables of the type found in Maria's and Anastasia's dresses. The ghoulish task paid a tidy dividend; the Bolsheviks collected nearly 18 pounds of diamonds and other precious stones. The burial party, having already desecrated the bodies, felt no compunction about further horribly mutilating them. After being hacked at, the now-unrecognizable forms were soaked in gasoline and burned. Most of what charred flesh remained after the incineration was dissolved when the bones were doused with acid. Very little was left of the dead when they were shoveled into a deep, water-filled pit. All the same, the Bolshevik guards took it upon themselves to drop several hand grenades into the hole to complete the process of erasing any remnant of Russia's last imperial dynasty.

Sometime later, the Bolshevik leader Leon Trotsky justified the gruesome murder of the Romanovs. "The execution of the Tsar's family was needed," Trotsky explained, "not only to frighten, horrify, and dishearten the enemy, but also in order to shake up [our] own ranks to show that there was no turning back."[9] To be sure, the point of no return had been reached and passed by the Russian revolutionaries led by men like Trotsky. From here forward, victory could be the only endpoint. History raced onward, carrying every Russian with it. No one really knew in what direction it would flow, but the tsar and the social order he had presided over were gone forever. What arose was a new Russia forged in the fires of revolution—the Bolshevik Revolution.

Old Russia

RUSSIA IN 1900

As the twentieth century dawned, Russia was in many ways a paradoxical land. The country was huge geographically, stretching from the Baltic Sea and Poland in the west to the Ural Mountains in the east. If one includes the Siberian land-mass, the Russian Empire in 1900 reached as far as the Pacific Ocean. North to south, Russia began in the frozen Arctic and spread southward into the Caucasus region and Central Asia. Yet for all this sheer size, the population was concentrated by and large in the farm villages of the "black soil" region of the south and, increasingly, near and in burgeoning cities such as St. Petersburg, Moscow, and Kiev.

Industry was rapidly taking center stage in the Russian economy, hence the growth of urban centers, but agriculture

A photo of an evening peasant supper in Russia, before the revolution. The plight of the peasantry was one of the chief sparks of the 1917 Bolshevik Revolution.

was still predominant. While Western Europe and the United States already had moved toward economies based upon factory production and mass consumption, Russia was just beginning its transformation to consumer capitalism. Russian factory output, it is true, increased by 8 percent between 1890 and 1899. The empire, moreover, had become the world's fourth largest producer of coal, iron, and steel; it ranked second only to the United States in oil. Russian mills churned out ever-larger amounts of textiles, food-processing equipment, rail cars, automobiles, and machine tools. Much of this material bounty was exported, but Russians living in the new urban centers were consuming increasing amounts at home. Yet for all this, 115 million of the total population of 127 million Russians still worked on farms, and food crop cultivation remained at the core of the Russian economy.

Culturally, Western tastes, trends, and ideas had deeply penetrated Russia by the end of the nineteenth century, but they faced stiff competition from the religious and social traditions to which many Russians clung. It was undeniable that large segments of the educated urban population had embraced Western European secularism and liberalism, while revolutionary ideologies first developed in France and Germany had taken firm root in the minds of Russian intellectuals. The vast majority of Russians, however, still followed the dictates of the Orthodox Church and the tsar, as their ancestors had done for centuries. Many Russians, especially among the rural peasantry, continued to shape their worldviews and belief systems according to the teachings of the Church and the proclamations of the tsarist bureaucracy. Submission and subordination to age-old authority were as commonplace in Russian farming villages and small towns as challenges to the same were in the cities. The idea of the tsar, in particular, occupied a special place among average Russians. As the historian Richard Pipes writes, the "loyalty [to the tsar] was a personal loyalty to the idealized image of a distant ruler whom [the Russian] saw as his terrestrial father and protector."[1] The familial analogy was intended to insulate the tsar against criticism and dissent, guaranteeing the continued loyalty of the people as children to their parent.

The Orthodox Church was similarly revered and, in the words of another scholar, Walter Laqueur, reinforced this loyalty to the state by functioning as "the handmaiden of the tsarist regime."[2] Obedience to the tsar, the Church told Russians, was obedience to God. Russians learned from the Church to accept tsarist absolutism as the will of God. Rebellion against one was rebellion against the other. Church and state together thus became earthly manifestations of a divine order. In return for its

A painting of a religious procession in the province of Kursk, circa 1880. The Russian Orthodox Church was enormously influential in pre-revolutionary Russia.

support, the tsarist state protected the Church from challenges to both its temporal and spiritual authority. It was a deal struck hundreds of years earlier, and one that both parties had adhered to ever since.

The Russian military, which supported both church and state with physical force, also was a contradictory mix of old and new. Among the largest in the world, the Russian army and navy were superficially comparable to their counterparts in Western Europe and had adopted many modern structures and techniques. Serious deficiencies, however, lurked within the military establishment, and these undermined its efficiency. The Russian officer corps, for one, was hidebound and inflexible. Made up of petty aristocrats with little more than a title to point to, the officer class was backward in its strategic thinking and weak in its tactical understanding of modern warfare. Most Russian officers also were thoroughly monarchist in their political tendencies, which made it difficult for them to accept political changes that might reduce the power of the tsar as commander in chief. Rank-and-file Russian soldiers and sailors, on the other hand, conscripted as they were from the urban working class and the rural peasantry, lacked any genuine attachment to the tsarist regime at all. These men performed their duties according to a military tradition of compulsory service they neither understood nor valued. Worse for their officers, common soldiers and sailors almost universally resented military discipline and usually hated the men who imposed it upon them.

Regressive and socially unstable, the Russian armed forces supported a tsarist edifice that was at once respected for its ancient origins and reviled for its corruption, inefficiency, and repressive inclinations. Tsar Nicholas II, who acceded to the throne in 1894 after his father's death from kidney disease, presided over a form of government that was composed of a set of antique institutions poorly suited to the requirements of twentieth-century politics and society. Beneath the tsar there existed the State Council, an advisory body with no practical authority or ability to check the actions of the monarch. Nicholas also had at hand a body known as the Council of Ministers, made up of government secretaries, provincial governors, and local prefects, but it similarly lacked any real influence in matters of state.

Ironically, the Russian government was more modern at the local than at the imperial level. Locally, two types of administrative bodies served the people. In rural areas, popularly elected *zemstvos*, or local councils, oversaw and regulated the operation of schools, road construction and maintenance, and public health. Municipal assemblies, known as *dumas*, did likewise in the larger towns and cities. Both zemstvos and dumas generally functioned smoothly and efficiently, representing the interests of the electorate in a manner incomprehensible to imperial officials sitting in St. Petersburg. These local institutions thus provided ordinary Russians with at least a rudimentary understanding of democracy and representative government.

YOUNG NICHOLAS II

Nicholas II was born into the Romanov dynasty on May 18, 1868. He could trace his family line back to the seventeenth century and the reign of Peter the Great. His father, Alexander III, expected great things of the newborn prince. The young Nicholas, however, proved to be a terrible disappointment to his father. He was a shy boy who spoke very little; Nicholas's feelings were easily hurt, and he possessed a compassionate streak that his father mocked relentlessly. Alexander III teased his son and often called him a girl in public. Nicholas's mother, Marie Fedorovna, however, indulged the boy and returned every kindness he showed to her. The royal mother and son shared an uncommon bond during Nicholas's childhood. It is hardly surprising, then, that when he grew into early manhood, Nicholas tried to replicate his relationship with his mother by marrying for love. Against the wishes of his father, who wanted a French match, Nicholas became engaged to Princess Alix of Hesse-Darmstadt, a granddaughter of England's Queen Victoria. Little known to either of the two, Alix had inherited the gene for hemophilia from her grandmother's line. She would pass it on to her son, Alexei, some 10 years later. When they wed, Nicholas was 21 years old and Alix, who eventually altered her first name to the more regal Alexandra, was only 17, but they were unquestionably in love with each other. They were married on November 15, 1894, just as Nicholas's life as the Russian tsar was beginning.

THE REFORM MOVEMENT

The contradictions and inequities of Russian life and society in 1900 amplified calls for reform that had been issuing from individual sources for at least 50 years. By the 1870s, these isolated voices of reform had merged into movements that demanded systematic alterations in the way Russians lived, worked, and were governed. Land and Freedom, an early socialist group, for example, sought land reform and a program for redistributing agricultural holdings to the peasantry. People's Freedom, a loose collection of radical reformers, gained recognition as one of the first groups in Russia to employ terrorist violence toward political ends. It proudly claimed responsibility for the 1881 assassination of Tsar Alexander II.

Among the reform groups, two in particular proved most influential and enduring—the Socialist Revolutionary Party (SR) and the Russian Social-Democratic Labor Party. Both organizations understood Russia's agrarian profile and thus the significance of the peasant class, but each aimed its propaganda and activities more broadly in the direction of the factory workers who comprised an expanding portion of the population. Underpaid, overworked, and often subjected to abusive and dangerous working conditions, these men and women turned out to be uniquely receptive to the socialist message espoused by the SRs and the Social Democrats. A political police report in 1901, in fact, noted with marked concern that socialist agitators "have achieved some success, unfortunately, in organizing the workers to fight against the government."[3] This was no small wonder given the fact that, by that year, an estimated 5,000 socialist cadres were at work in Russia trying to convince the working class to reject the capitalist economic order and the tsarist regime that nourished and protected it.

Whether SR or Social Democrat, most of the revolutionary operatives preaching to the Russian workers identified themselves as Marxists. Drawing on the theories of the German philosopher Karl Marx, they believed that the industrial capitalist system represented simply one stage of development in a global evolutionary process moving first toward socialism, then toward a dictatorship of the working class, and then toward Communism, a stateless social order in which every person worked and reaped the fruits of society's collective labor. The job of the revolutionary, it followed, was to guide Russia's peasants and factory workers through the difficult transition from capitalism to socialism, thus establishing the preconditions for Communism. Socialist Revolutionaries and Social Democrats alike took this to be true. Most members of both parties also held that the change from one historical stage to the next would take place spontaneously and without violence, once a certain developmental threshold had been reached. Global political evolution, they felt certain, was an inevitable series of events that needed neither manipulation nor bloodshed to unfold.

THE BOLSHEVIKS ARE BORN

A minority of Marxists, however, primarily within the Social-Democratic Labor Party, disagreed strongly with this idea. This small but growing faction argued that the working class, or the proletariat as it was called, required immediate and professional leadership in its upcoming battle with the capitalist elite, or bourgeoisie. Among this new breed of Marxist socialist revolutionary was a young man named Vladimir Ilich Ulyanov. Born in Simbirsk in April 1870, Ulyanov recalled his brother being hanged in 1887 his for alleged involvement in the assassination of Alexander II and a thwarted bomb attack aimed at eliminating the entire royal family. From that point forward, Ulyanov dedicated himself to bringing down the monarchy, which he blamed for his brother's death, and to bringing justice to Russia. Arrested for his own political activities and expelled while at university, Ulyanov spent over a year in prison before being exiled to Siberia. The life of a state prisoner, contrary to the intentions of his captors, only further radicalized the young socialist. This prompted him to escape to Switzerland in 1900. Now a fugitive from the law, Ulyanov thought it best to assume a false identity; he began going by the name Vladimir Lenin.

Writing under this name, Lenin penned his first great work of Marxist revolutionary literature in 1902, *What Is to Be Done?* In this extended essay, Lenin drafted a blueprint for the creation of a proletarian dictatorship (rule by the working class) and eventual socialist state in Russia, from which revolution would then be exported around the world. Lenin argued that in Russia, "we must come to the positive conclusion that a strong revolutionary organization is absolutely necessary."[4] Refining this proposition further, Lenin called for the formation of "a party which unites into one inseparable whole the assault on the government in the name of the entire people," an assault led by "professional revolutionaries . . . the real political leaders of the entire people."[5]

A year after writing these words, Lenin presented his tentative revolutionary program to the delegates of the 1903 Social-Democratic Labor Party Congress. Since he was deviating from traditional Marxism, Lenin was challenged to describe how he planned to effect his revolution. The response was simple—violent overthrow by mobilizing the Russian masses. Most of the delegates flatly rejected Lenin's notions, but enough of them sided with Lenin to give his faction control over the editorial board of the party newspaper, *Iskra*. Because his opponents represented a minority on the board, they were labeled *men'shinstvo*, or the minority; Lenin's comrades were thus known as *bol'shinstvo*, or the majority. Over the next 15 years, the Mensheviks would uphold the traditional Marxist worldview, in contrast to the more radical one embraced by Lenin and what were now called his Bolsheviks.

The First Russian
Revolution

THE RUSSO-JAPANESE WAR

As Lenin began building his Bolshevik faction into a revolutionary force, Tsar Nicholas II was complaining that he had "to carry the burden of a terrible responsibility" for the security and prosperity of the Russian state.[1] In January 1904, that burden grew far heavier, as war with imperial Japan broke out in the northern Chinese region of Manchuria. The tsar, according to tradition, personally announced to the Russian people the opening of hostilities. He did so, however, from the Winter Palace in St. Petersburg rather than from the ancient walled fortress of the Kremlin in Moscow, as had been customary for Russian monarchs. Many Russians believed that this breach of protocol boded ill for the imperial war effort; others, however, were more confident. Russian newspapers heaped racial scorn on the Japanese and demanded that the "insolent Asiatics" be taught a proper lesson in humility.[2] Initially, the public mood reflected the upbeat tenor of such pronouncements, but that soon changed. The war dragged on, month after bloody month. Russian battlefield defeats mounted, as the Japanese Army penetrated deeper into Manchuria. Accompanying the dark news from the front were food and fuel shortages at home caused by the war. Inflation ran rampant as demand for staples and consumer goods rapidly outstripped supply. Soaring prices drained the finances of ordinary Russians. Resentment grew, as did a gnawing sense that the tsar's government was unable or unwilling to remedy the situation.

Liberal reformers began issuing calls for immediate action in the shape of political change, and moderate socialists soon joined them. The Union of Liberation, founded in 1904, demanded nationwide elections and the creation of a representative assembly with the power to mend the economy and stop the war. Radical socialists, chief among them the Bolsheviks, went even further and began hinting at possible revolutionary action to bring about the needed changes. Groups and individuals already had emerged that were not shy about using violence to further their aims. These men sometimes gathered themselves together into loosely structured fighting organizations associated with one or another socialist party. Occasionally they operated alone. When one radical assassinated the interior minister, the Bolsheviks hailed the attack as a sign that the people were ready for an armed seizure of power by the working class. The St. Petersburg Bolsheviks, in particular, wanted to act. On December 19, 1904, the Bolshevik committee in the capital wrote to Lenin begging for more support: "You have no idea how critical the situation in Russia is just now. . . . Demands for [Bolshevik cadres] are coming in from all over. . . . We need people. Everybody is asking."[3] Lenin did not respond.

Many Bolsheviks were determined to begin preparing for revolution, even though it was clear that the working class they

A photo of a Russian six-inch howitzer battery taken at the defense of Port Arthur during the Russo-Japanese War (1904–1905). The embarrassing string of defeats inflicted on the Russians increased dissatisfaction with the tsarist government and provided a major cause of the 1905 Russian Revolution.

intended to empower was not yet ready to rise up against the tsarist order and smash the monarchy. Segments of it, however, were ready to organize their ranks for peaceful collective action. The first to do so were the factory workers in St. Petersburg. Using the model of a fraternal organization, a group of laborers in the Russian capital came together as the Assembly of St. Petersburg Factory Workers, under the leadership of a reformist priest, Father Georgii Gapon, to urge Nicholas II to improve the lot of working people by repairing the Russian economy and ending the war.

BLOODY SUNDAY

Yet the war against Japan went on, and so did the failure of the Russian armies. Day by day, the prospect of victory faded as utter defeat became more likely. On the home front, the anger and frustration of the Russian people rose, along with skyrocketing costs of food and fuel. The scarcity of common staples bore down on average Russians, workers and peasants alike. The flashpoint of the tensions was reached in January 1905, when 150,000 workers took to the streets, led by Father Gapon, to demand labor reforms and an end to the war. The current leadership, Gapon claimed, "has devastated the country, has involved it in a horrible war, and is leading it further and further into ruin. . . . Popular representation is essential. The people must help themselves and govern themselves."[4] Heartened by the workers' obvious willingness to stand up for themselves, Gapon announced his intention to organize a march to the Winter Palace, where Nicholas II was tending his now-pregnant wife, in order to deliver his protest document to the tsar in person.

The capital's Bolshevik and Menshevik committees took lukewarm stands on Gapon's plan. The Mensheviks and their SR allies offered grudging support but little else. The Bolsheviks, with Lenin in exile, opposed the march in both theory and practice. Lenin, in fact, forbade his party from any participation at all. "Freedom isn't bought at so cheap a price as one petition," Lenin wrote in a telegram to his followers, "even if presented by a priest in the workers' name."[5] The Bolshevik leaders ordered party members to stand down and await further instructions, despite frantic pleas for action. As was the case the previous December, Bolsheviks in St. Petersburg begged for trained cadres. "We are running the risk of losing one city after another for the lack of people," wrote one operative in the capital. "Every day I get heaps of letters from various places imploring [us] to send people."[6] Lenin was unmoved—no collaboration would be allowed. The Bolshevik chief himself would follow events from Switzerland, where he kept up on developments by reading local Swiss newspapers.

Effectively abandoned by the moderate and radical factions of the Social-Democratic Labor Party, Gapon, his strikers, and their families gathered together on the afternoon of Sunday, January 9. Converging on the Winter Palace from several directions at once, Gapon's columns made for Palace Square, where they were supposed to meet at 2:00 P.M. The processions, as promised, were orderly and peaceful, but, more than that, they were reflective of the traditional attachments the Russian people still harbored to the Orthodox Church and the tsar. As they moved toward the palace, marchers held aloft banners proclaiming their love for the tsar notwithstanding their disappointment in his government's policies. Some also carried Nicholas's portrait along with the national flag. Other workers cradled religious icons or crucifixes in their arms. From nearly every column, voices arose singing church hymns or reciting prayers. Gapon's protesters wanted the tsar to know that they advocated reform, not revolution.

In the heart of St. Petersburg, near the Narva Arch, a monument to Russia's triumph over Napoleon, the line of marchers with Gapon at its head was brought to a halt by tsarist troops. The commander of the soldiers instructed the workers and their families to disperse immediately or suffer the consequences for challenging the regime. The demonstrators refused to comply. Instead, they pushed forward. Under strict orders to prevent the workers from reaching the royal palace, the officer once again told them to turn back. Getting no positive response from the people or Gapon, the commander ordered his men to open fire. Eight successive volleys of rifle fire later, 10 workers lay dead in the snow and dozens ran or crawled away wounded.

Similar tragic scenarios played out all over St. Petersburg on Bloody Sunday. By evening, the death toll had reached 96 dead and 333 wounded, of whom 34 would later die from their injuries. Gapon, now a hunted man, fled to Finland, where he was murdered a year later. His petition to the tsar, so humble in its sentiment and so costly in innocent blood, was never delivered. Informed that his soldiers had shot down hundreds of his loyal subjects, Nicholas could only mourn, "a grim day! . . . God, how sad and grim!"[7]

THE OCTOBER MANIFESTO

The public reaction to the Bloody Sunday massacre came swiftly and was nearly unanimous in its condemnation of the shootings. "Tsar Nicholas," a liberal newspaper editorial proclaimed, "has revealed himself as the enemy and butcher of the people."[8] A socialist pamphlet issued soon after the events of January 9 put its denunciation in slogan form: "Down with the Tsar-murderer! Down with autocracy! Long live social democracy! . . . Long live the revolution!"[9] Nicholas, stung by the severity of the criticism directed at him personally, responded with contempt. "I know that the workman's life is not easy," the tsar said condescendingly, "[but] to come in a mutinous crowd to apprise me of your needs—that is criminal."[10] The tsar rejected the complaints of the St. Petersburg workers and dismissed their protests as the product of agitation by "ill-intentioned leaders" who wanted to establish in the motherland a "form of government, alien to Our country."[11] The tsar accepted no responsibility whatsoever for the state terror unleashed on the Sunday marchers.

In his ignorance and denial, Nicholas failed to notice that the strikes begun by Gapon and the Putilov workers continued after the brutal suppression of January 9. Far from bringing the stoppages to an end, Bloody Sunday only served to energize those pushing for substantial reforms, and thus contributed to the spread of the strikes far beyond the confines of the St. Petersburg industrial district. Factory workers struck in Moscow, Kiev, Warsaw, the Baltic cities, Central Asia, and the Caucasus. By February, 500,000 industrial workers already on strike were joined by more than 7,000 students from Moscow and St. Petersburg who had refused to attend classes in order to show their solidarity with the laborers. Teachers, independent scholars, journalists, lawyers, and doctors in both cities soon made common cause with the workers and students. Provincial zemstvos and municipal dumas (respectively, the local councils and town governments) throughout Russia passed resolutions demanding immediate imperial reforms. Here and there in the countryside, peasant uprisings broke out. Farmers began to call for sweeping changes in land tenure policies and in the redistribution of agricultural property currently held by the aristocracy and the bourgeois elite.

On May Day 1905, massive demonstrations held across the country provoked counterdemonstrations and violent attacks by tsarist thugs known as the Black Hundred. A mixed bag of petty criminals, racists, religious fanatics, and heavy-drinking street toughs, the Black Hundred targeted those who in any way challenged the status quo of the Church and the tsar. Encouraged by imperial bureaucrats, local officials, and Orthodox clergymen, the gangs beat and openly murdered liberals, socialists, and strikers. Anyone suspected of participating in labor actions or even giving moral support to the workers' cause was likely to feel the fists and boots of the Black Hundred. Special hatred and violence, however, were reserved for the minority that was traditionally held in the lowest regard and was perennially blamed for all of Russia's ills: the Jews. Using the strikes as an excuse to vent their extreme anti-Semitism, Black Hundred mobs descended on every Jew they could find, politically active or not.

Reviled by the tsar and subjected to a campaign of state-sanctioned terror, reformers and radicals alike prepared to move to a new level of action. The revolutionary tension finally broke on May 14, 1905, when news reached Russia that an imperial fleet sent to retake Port Arthur—Russia's main naval base, seized by the Japanese at the war's outset—had been

An engraving taken from the Italian newspaper *La Domenica del Corriere* of the battleship *Potemkin* bombarding the port of Odessa, Russia. The crew of the *Potemkin* mutinied against their tsarist officers in 1905.

destroyed by the Japanese in the Tsushima Straits off the coast of Korea. Support for the tsar's government collapsed. Street fighting broke out in Kharkov, Baku, and Odessa, where 2,000 people died before martial law was declared on June 15. That same day, the sailors on the battleship *Potemkin* mutinied and commandeered their ship, steaming it toward Odessa and firing two shells at the city before eventually abandoning it near the port of Constanza in Romania and fleeing.

By the late summer of 1905, strikes had paralyzed nearly every aspect of social life in Russia. Violence was flaring up across the empire. Soldiers and sailors looked with increasing favor upon the actions taken by the *Potemkin*'s crew; reports of sporadic refusals by enlisted men to obey orders began coming in to the imperial military headquarters. Russia stood on the verge of national chaos. Nicholas had no choice but to relent. On August 6, the tsar announced that elections would be held the following January for representatives who would sit in a new state duma, which was designed to serve Nicholas as a popular advisory body. Seventeen days later, Nicholas's commissioner to the peace talks with the Japanese, who was being hosted by U.S. President Theodore Roosevelt in Portsmouth, New Hampshire, cabled St. Petersburg that there had been a breakthrough in the negotiations. Given certain concessions on Russia's part, Japan was willing to sign a treaty ending the war. One of the main causes of the popular upheavals had been eliminated.

The promised elections and the Treaty of Portsmouth should have been enough to satisfy those calling for change in Russia. Instead, the civil unrest not only continued, but worsened. Bolsheviks, Mensheviks, and SRs urged the Russian people to boycott the January elections as a sham; furthermore, Bolsheviks told workers and students to demonstrate against any state duma set up to rubber-stamp the tsar's decisions. In the streets, the walkouts that had begun in January expanded and merged into a general strike, including nearly every category of worker from pharmacists to chocolate makers. By October, the St. Petersburg workers felt confident enough to form a representative assembly of their own to help organize and lead the nationwide labor action. It was christened the St. Petersburg Soviet of Workers' Deputies, simply known as the Soviet, and it threatened to become a competitor for the

proposed state duma, if not an actual revolutionary government in its own right.

The Mensheviks and SRs enthusiastically supported the
Soviet and sought to pack it with their own members. The
Bolsheviks only reluctantly agreed to take part. "Circumstances
may force us to participate" in the Soviet, Lenin wrote to his
cadres in St. Petersburg, but he reminded them that "such
participation is admissible only if [Bolshevik] independence
. . . is fully protected."[12] Privately, Lenin sneered at the Soviet.
He mocked it as one of those "politically amorphous and
socialistically immature workers' organizations" that could
serve no genuine revolutionary purpose.[13] Rather than throw-
ing in with other leftist groups, Lenin reminded his Bolshevik
comrades not to confuse "the democratic and the socialist
overturn—the struggle for a republic . . . and the struggle for

THE OCTOBER MANIFESTO

The October Manifesto began the process of redefining
Russian politics and society. Dated October 17, 1905, the
manifesto emanated directly from Nicholas II himself (here
speaking in the formal first-person plural that was typical of
imperial proclamations) and read:

Disturbances and unrest in the capitals and in many places
of Our Empire fill Our heart with a great and painful grief. .
. . Out of the present disturbances there may grow a serious
popular disorder and a threat to the integrity and unity of Our
Empire. The great oath of Imperial service requires that, with
all the force of Our intelligence and authority, and as quickly
as possible, We bring to an end disturbances perilous to the
state. Having ordered the appropriate authorities to take

socialism."[14] He also warned his Bolsheviks against any devia-
tion from his orders, stressing the need for their "unquestioning
obedience."[15] The Bolshevik Revolution would come, but not
now, and not through compromise with either the Mensheviks
or the Soviet.

Faced with open defiance and a likely parallel government
to his own, Nicholas bent once again. The tsar issued a proclamation that acknowledged the civil rights of ordinary Russians,
safeguarded political liberty, and provided for a duma with
legislative authority—albeit one that was quite limited relative
to parliaments in Western Europe. This October Manifesto,
however brief and rather vague, marked imperial Russia's tentative first step toward the kind of representative government and
limited monarchy that reformers had imagined for decades. The
Bolsheviks, however, were not satisfied. The manifesto, in their

steps against open acts of disorder, riot, and violence, so as
to protect peaceful people who seek quietly to perform their
duty, We, in order to carry out the general policies outlined
by Us for quieting the life of the nation, have found it necessary to unify the activities of the central government.

What followed was a list of freedoms, including those of
conscience, speech, assembly, and association, and a promise of elections to a representative parliament. Nicholas
concluded the manifesto by calling "on all faithful sons of
Russia to remember their duty to their Fatherland, to assist
in putting an end to these unprecedented disturbances, and
to exert with Us all their power to restore quiet and peace
to Our native land."*

*Sidney Harcave, **First Blood: The Russian Revolution of 1905.**
New York: Macmillan and Company, 1964, pp. 195-196.

thinking, was nothing more than a small concession thrown to the masses to quiet them and to allow the state to survive the turmoil in the streets. Leon Trotsky, a future Bolshevik leader, dismissed the manifesto as an empty gesture. "A constitution is given," Trotsky scoffed, "but the autocracy remains. Everything is given—and nothing is given."[16]

OLD RUSSIA REACTS

The October Manifesto came as a relief to most Russians, even those who had agitated for more extensive changes, but not to the Bolsheviks. Returning from exile in November 1905, Lenin demanded that the Soviet ignore the manifesto and reconfigure itself into a true revolutionary government that represented the interests of Russia's workers, peasants, soldiers, sailors, and socialist intelligentsia. The Bolshevik leader wanted the Soviet to seize the moment and use it to initiate a socialist revolution in Russia that would reverberate throughout Europe and start a chain reaction of overthrow and upheaval that would usher in a new order around the world. At first, the deputies sitting in St. Petersburg rejected Lenin's plea, but Bolshevik influence in the Soviet managed to grow rapidly. The tsar's ministers—seeing the potential danger in any further radicalization of the reform movement in general and the Soviet in particular—moved aggressively to check the Bolsheviks and their sympathizers among the Menshevik and SR far left. Drawing on recent experience, the government released the terror of the Black Hundred once again.

For about a month, Russians had enjoyed what the reformers called the Days of Freedom, a period of political liberty hitherto unknown in the empire. The government reaction now brought these days to an abrupt and violent halt. The members of the St. Petersburg Soviet were arrested en masse in December. The Moscow Soviet, modeled on the one in the Russian capital, was dispersed and forbidden to reconvene. The smaller provincial soviets that had sprung up across Russia were likewise broken up. Waves of arbitrary arrests swept up Bolsheviks and other radicals and carried them off to prison or into exile. Lenin, on several police lists and perhaps even slated for assassination, fled to Switzerland once again. He would not return home for another 12 years.

Given tacit permission to spread fear throughout the land, the Black Hundred went to work with abandon. Beatings and killings became commonplace in some areas of the country, as Black Hundred toughs took vengeance upon and meted out vigilante justice to those they saw as being threats to Mother Russia, its Orthodox Church, and its tsar. As in the past, the Jewish people were a prime target. In the city of Tomsk, 200 people, mostly Jews and known Bolsheviks, were slain; in Odessa, 700 Jews died. A further 700 Jews were murdered in other cities and towns by killers who had the support of local governments and religious leaders. Thugs savagely persecuted Jews and Bolsheviks. They eventually blended the two sets of victims into a single new menace they labeled Jewish Bolshevism. Tsar Nicholas himself publicly blamed the "strong reaction" of the Black Hundred and others like them on the fact that, among the radicals, "nine-tenths of the troublemakers are Jews."[17] That was why, the tsar continued, "the people's anger turned against" the Jews and "some Russian agitators . . . [who] suffered as well."[18]

Thus the first Russian Revolution ended with concessions to the popular will on the one hand and violent repression on the other. The cauldron of civil unrest and radical action now would simmer until stirred once again by the hand of war and economic turmoil.

The Fall of the House of Romanov

RUSSIA AND THE FIRST WORLD WAR

Far from slowing, the pace of political, economic, and social change in Russia quickened after the 1905 revolution, notwithstanding the best efforts of Tsar Nicholas II, the Orthodox Church, and Russian conservatives seeking to freeze the empire in time. Stark political repression, more than anything else, indicated the degree to which the Russian government remained tethered to the past. As before, dissent was uniformly suppressed. Socialists, in particular, came under attack by the tsar's secret police as they sought to address the needs of the industrial workers and the peasantry. The imperial perspective on socialist organizers, according to a former police director in 1907, was simple. The tsarist regime viewed the process of governing as a clash of mutually exclusive absolutes: "[T]here are the people and there is state authority . . . the latter is under constant threat from the former, for which reason it is subject to protective measures."[1] Arrest, imprisonment, and exile were employed freely by the police; these measures reduced the number of avowed Marxists in Russia from an estimated 150,000 in 1907 to a mere 10,000 by 1910. Among this group, Bolsheviks were singled out by the authorities for special attention, in an effort to halt the growth of this especially dangerous political organization.

The oppression meted out by the regime, however, worked against itself. The tsarist assault on the left only energized men and women determined to reform—if not fundamentally restructure—Russian politics. Socialist revolutionaries repositioned themselves as radical Marxists seeking the immediate formation of a workers' state, albeit via the democratic process. The Menshevik faction of the Social-Democratic Party continued to advocate for socialist change only when the historical conditions were right. Until then, the Mensheviks were content to compromise with bourgeois liberals in the Duma. The Bolsheviks, meanwhile, differed from their fellow socialists in their insistence that any revolutionary action must come at the earliest possible political moment and, as a necessity, had to involve violence. Lenin believed that "the bourgeois state . . . cannot be replaced by . . . withering away, but, as a general rule, only through a violent revolution."[2] For the Bolsheviks, only armed violence held the promise of completely erasing capitalism and tsarism together. The divide between the Mensheviks and the Bolsheviks grew so wide, in fact, that their continued coexistence within a single political party became impossible. In 1911, the two factions officially separated and became distinct parties in their own rights. The Bolsheviks were now free of all restraint.

By 1914, Russia could be described as being in a state of profound tension. No one could confidently predict the empire's political future. Nor could anyone at the time appreciate the full impact of the tsar's decision to enter the First World War as part of an alliance that included Great Britain, France, Italy, and eventually the United States. Opposing these Allies were the Central Powers of Germany, Austria-Hungary, and Turkey. Among these nations, powerful Germany was the most feared by the Russians. Past tsars had admired Germany and had often tried to emulate German ways, but in 1914, Nicholas II wanted none of that. In order to highlight Russia's belligerence, he ordered the name of the imperial capital to be changed from the Germanic St. Petersburg to the more Slavic Petrograd.

From the newly christened Petrograd, Tsar Nicholas led Russia into its second war in just 10 years. But this would be no ordinary war for empire. It would be a total war, one that required total commitment on the part of the Russian state and the Russian people. The inherent stresses and strains of such a conflict contained enough negative power to break a fragile nation like Russia. Nicholas was willing to gamble that his subjects would be able to endure. He was convinced that ordinary Russians loved him, were devoted to their country, and could withstand the rigors of a global war.

The tsar's confidence was soon put to the test. Russia and Germany went to war on August 1, 1914. Less than a month later, the German army inflicted a staggering defeat upon Nicholas's forces at the Battle of Tannenberg. Two weeks after that, another Russian command was crushed at the Masurian Lakes. Russia's combined losses in men and matériel for August and September 1914 topped 250,000 men and more than 650 artillery pieces. From the outset, Russia was losing the war. Yet battlefield defeats represented only one terrible reality in that first year of World War I. At home, the Russian people once again suffered through wartime shortages of food, fuel, and transport. The shift in industrial production from consumer goods to military hardware was felt as a sharp drop in the national standard of living. The demand for factory labor com-

pounded Russia's problems by swelling the already burgeoning urban population. Workers needed to be fed, clothed, and
housed as they strived to equip the tsarist armies. Bread, meat,
coal, oil, and soon housing supplies, as a consequence, rapidly
dwindled.

By mid-1915, Russia was in retreat from the German divisions and experiencing urban and rural unrest at home. Peasants
endured long, hard days of labor in the fields only to have their
grain seized by troops who left little or no surplus behind.
Hunger became commonplace once more. The military draft
also weighed heavily on a peasantry dependent upon male workers on the land. Thus, both the crops and the young men who
tilled the soil to raise them were swept up in the service of the
tsar. The stage already was set for starvation and discontent when
the 1916 harvest failed. The worst grain crop in a decade left
Russians in the cities and in the countryside more disillusioned
and angry than at any time since 1905.

THE TSAR'S RESPONSE

Sitting comfortably in Switzerland, Lenin watched with some
satisfaction as the tsarist order slowly imploded. The fact that
the capitalist countries were ripping one another to pieces in the
trenches that scarred Western Europe confirmed Lenin's belief
that the Bolsheviks' new day was coming. But it was the loom-
ing chaos in Russia that gave the Bolshevik leader real hope for
an imminent homecoming and a rapid seizure of power. Lenin
did not fully appreciate how the tsar's weakness had energized
the Mensheviks as well. The Bolsheviks' nemesis was similarly
eyeing a move against Nicholas's government.

The pressure of German boots marching toward the
Russian heartland widened all of the existing fissures in tsarist
society and created more than a few new ones. The Russian
Army's general staff proved to be hopelessly incompetent. The
seemingly endless stream of defeats exposed the paper-thin
loyalty and low morale of the imperial troops. Worse still, the

impending crisis found the Russian government, in particular the tsar himself, utterly paralyzed by the magnitude of the approaching disaster. No one in the Winter Palace seemed capable of implementing measures that might improve life at home or the performance of the army on the front.

The tsar's response to military calamity, economic collapse, and a revival of socialist opposition was indeed pathetic. Rather than acting boldly, Nicholas retreated inward and sought counsel from the worst sources—ignorant advisers, such as his wife Alexandra, corrupt bureaucrats, and obvious frauds. Perhaps the most devious and destructive of these advisers was a crude charlatan named Grigory Rasputin. Priest, mystic, and sexual deviant, Rasputin entered the royal household upon the dubious claim that he possessed the requisite skills to cure the imperial heir, Alexei, of his hemophilia. Rasputin masterfully played on the hopes and fears of Nicholas and Alexandra. In time, he came to be a trusted confidant of the tsar. Nicholas increasingly turned to Rasputin concerning matters of state, a practice that enraged the tsar's traditional inner circle. In 1916, Prince Lvov, for example, derided the employment of "secret medicine men and magicians in our state administration."[3] No one could mistake to whom the prince referred.

Rasputin, for his part, reveled in his newfound glory and influence. The dark-eyed, bearded monk used his closeness to the Romanovs to enrich himself and satisfy his desires for alcohol and women. Eventually, he took his schemes too far; in late 1916, Rasputin was murdered by a group of men led by a distant member of the royal family. Nicholas reacted to the assassination by flying into a blind rage that blended into a fit of paranoia. The tsar, from 1916 on, withdrew into his palace and his family. He trusted no one and refused to listen to, let alone consult, his staff. Nicholas turned an especially cold shoulder to the State Duma and the reform advocates. He became convinced that they were all part of a radical plot to bring down the Romanov dynasty.

A photo of Russian mystic Grigory Rasputin (seated, with beard) surrounded by some of his admirers. Rasputin exercised considerable power over the tsar and tsarina, partly due to their belief in his ability to heal their son's hemophilia. Because Rasputin's influence over the House of Romanov was widely unpopular, he was murdered by Prince Felix Yusupov and Grand Duke Dmitri Romanov in December 1916.

THE FEBRUARY REVOLUTION

By January 1917, Tsar Nicholas II was living in a fog of distrust and fear. There "no longer [was] a government," according to Prince Lvov.[4] The State Duma was ineffectual at best. The state ministers had been muzzled by a tsar who did not want to hear from them at all. The Bolsheviks celebrated every increase in Nicholas's personal management of national affairs. Every mistake tied him more closely to failures on the battlefield and in the streets. Despite Lenin's exile and the absence of many key leaders, the Bolshevik Petrograd Committee intensified its activity in the early weeks of 1917. The Bolsheviks spied

on their Menshevik and SR opponents and infiltrated workers' groups and peasant collectives. Bolshevik cadres had been
painstakingly positioned to take advantage of the earliest revolutionary opportunity.

Lenin, however, as he had in 1905, ordered his comrades in
Petrograd to proceed carefully and quietly. The Bolsheviks at
home were given strict guidelines, which stated that cooperation with other socialist groups, trade unions, and reformers
was forbidden. As a consequence, Bolshevik influence among
the masses and the party's ability to manipulate public opinion
remained slight. The overall result of Lenin's stubbornness was
that the Bolsheviks ceded the political stage to the Mensheviks,
SRs, and moderates at the very moment that the tsar's administration was beginning to disintegrate.

At the end of January 1917, Tsar Nicholas decided he would
dissolve the State Duma and not hold new elections. The events
that followed only reinforced his conviction to do away with
popular representatives and to again rule Russia directly. After
another labor dispute at the Putilov Works, the company man-
agers fired several prominent union leaders; the workers immediately went on strike. On February 23, the tsar returned from a
depressing visit to the imperial headquarters at Mogilev to find
new food shortages and an additional 90,000 Petrograd workers on the streets rather than in the factories. Even more trou-
bling were reports that sporadic violence had broken out in the
city's streets. Worse challenges to the tsar's authority, however,
were brewing. Nicholas, more defiant than ever after his trip to
Mogilev, reacted with uncharacteristic speed and determination.
"I command you," the tsar ordered his officers in the Petrograd
Military District, "to put an end as from tomorrow to all disturbances in the streets of the capital."[5] Consequently, the garrison
commander sent his men into the streets. His rules of engage-
ment were simple: If confronted by striking workers, "give a
warning signal three times and after the third signal open fire."[6]

Within hours, the commander's orders were carried out.
Meeting a group of strikers on the street, an army officer was

A photo of demonstrators gathering in front of the Winter Palace during the 1917 Russian Revolution.

shot while attempting to grab a red banner from the hands of a factory worker. Troops moved out in response and, near the Winter Palace, they opened fire on a crowd of people; 40 workers were killed or badly wounded in the encounter. Retreating, the workers hurled insults at the soldiers responsible for the bloodshed and accused them of cutting down their own kind. The troops, shamed by the stain of innocent blood on their hands, returned to their barracks, where they debated whether or not to obey further orders to shoot strikers. Their discussions led the men to the conclusion that their place was with the people of Petrograd. That same day, thousands of imperial soldiers defected to the side of the demonstrators, taking their firearms with them.

The revolutionary events of February 1917 now unfolded in a blur of political maneuvering and street action. On February

26, the now-armed and confident workers resurrected the old St. Petersburg Soviet as the Petrograd Soviet of Workers' and Soldiers' Deputies. A mutiny broke out hours later in the imperial barracks, and even more troops left to join the now 240,000 striking workers railing against poor labor conditions and the tsarist government. With the addition of the soldiers, the list of popular grievances grew to include the war and Nicholas's failures as a political leader. What began as labor unrest now had been transformed into a broader political protest. As the soldiers had done before them, the sailors of the Baltic Fleet stationed at Kronstadt soon swung behind the workers and joined the people in carrying painted, handmade red banners calling for change.

Rightly fearing that his power was fading under the relentless popular assault, the tsar announced his decision to disband the State Duma. To everyone's amazement, it refused. Instead, on February 28, the Duma established a committee to act as the Provisional Government of Russia. Its declared purpose was to save what was left of state authority and bring order to the nation. The self-proclaimed government called for an immediate election to set up a Russian parliament, the Constituent Assembly, and hinted at the abdication of Tsar Nicholas himself. The Provisional Government, thanks to Lenin's stubborn refusal to allow his Bolsheviks a role in what he imagined to be a bourgeois scheme, quickly gave over its leadership to moderate reformers, SRs, and Mensheviks. Petrograd's Bolsheviks, much to their frustration, assumed the part of spectators in the meantime.

An army dispatch on March 1 summed up the situation in Russia as the Provisional Government openly challenged Nicholas for power: "[W]e received from Petrograd one telegram after another depicting a revolutionary moment in full swing. . . . Unrest broke out in Moscow and other important centres. . . . Abdication, it was said, was the only way out."[7] Russia stood on the brink of a popular uprising unlike anything in its history. If the workers, soldiers, and Provisional Government had their way, Nicholas would face the quite real possibility of presiding over the simultaneous destruction of the monarchy and the loss of the war. Should the Germans launch an offensive, the internal turmoil of the moment might even result in the foreign occupation of the motherland. For Nicholas II, this was too much. Despite his faults, the tsar still loved Russia and took seriously his duty to preserve it. Thus, after extensive talks with his brother, Grand Duke Michael, and representatives of the Provisional Government, Nicholas agreed to step down on March 2. He then surprised his friends and enemies alike by rejecting the crown for his son, Alexei, as well; Grand Duke Michael would become the new tsar. On March 3, Nicholas signed the abdication documents and left the throne to the grand duke, who wisely refused it in turn. Michael had little choice, even if he had felt up to the job of ruling a nation that was in disarray. According to the president of the Duma, "the Grand Duke would have reigned only a few hours. . . . [He] would have been killed immediately."[8] Or, like his predecessor, he would have found himself under arrest. Nicholas II, his wife, and their son and daughters were taken into custody shortly after the tsar relinquished the crown. Within a matter of hours, the centuries-old Romanov dynasty had fallen.

Russia was now in the hands of a collection of reformers, democrats, SRs, and Mensheviks—exactly the type of politicians so reviled by Lenin and the Bolsheviks. Yet, according to Lenin's strict orders, Petrograd's Bolshevik Committee did nothing but watch as the Provisional Government took control of Russia and made overtures toward the Soviet concerning a political alliance. Toward this end, the Provisional Government, officially headed by Prince Lvov but really managed by the Socialist Revolutionary minister of justice, Alexander Kerensky, issued its program. The 8-Point Proclamation outlined the new administration's vision for Russia: a guarantee of full civil rights; amnesty for all political prisoners, even those convicted of terrorist offenses; an end to ethnic and religious discrimination; the replacement of the police with a popular militia; and a real parliament elected by the people. Most importantly for the

ALEXANDER KERENSKY

Although Alexander Fyodorovich Kerensky became Lenin's fiercest political opponent, the men shared a great deal in common. Like Lenin, Kerensky had been born in Simbirsk to a father who had built a career in education. In fact, Kerensky's father had been the headmaster at the school where Lenin had studied as a boy, and the two families knew one another well. Born on May 2, 1881, Kerensky was the younger of the two men. Unlike Lenin, he had family connections to the Orthodox Church; his grandfather and an uncle were Orthodox priests. Kerensky also differed from Lenin in his attraction to traditional Marxism, which counseled a slow, methodical approach to bringing about the transition from capitalism to socialism and eventually to Communism. Trained as a lawyer, Kerensky was thus in a good position to become a leader of the Socialist Revolutionaries and a popular figure among Mensheviks. Furthermore, his education in law made him the perfect candidate for the job of justice minister in the Provisional Government. After the Bolshevik Revolution, Kerensky lived abroad, first in Finland, then in Germany, France, the United States, Australia, and the United States again. He resumed his career and eventually taught at Stanford University, while writing several books on the Russian revolutions and the Bolshevik movement. Kerensky's personal life after 1917 was similarly busy; he married twice and had two sons who went on to successful careers in engineering. Alexander Kerensky died in New York on June 6, 1970, and was buried in London, England.

new government, troops were to be assured of the same civil liberties as other Russians, and the Petrograd garrison was not to be transferred out of the capital for any reason.

Kerensky, the SRs, the Mensheviks, and their allies in the Soviet had stated their ends clearly. The Bolsheviks countered by taking an even more radical stance. Their refusal to collaborate with other groups did not mean that the Bolsheviks had ended their bid for power. On the contrary, they countered the Provisional Government's proclamation with one of their own. In it, the Bolsheviks openly appealed to the sympathies of many in the Soviet as well as those that were common in the soldiers' and sailors' barracks. Lenin, still living in Switzerland, sought to undermine the Provisional Government while it was still vulnerable, and he knew a forceful Bolshevik statement concerning Russia's political future might do just that. *Pravda*, the party newspaper, thus published Lenin's Order No. 1 on March 7. It called for a permanent shift of authority from the government to the Soviet and, through their membership in the Soviet, to Russia's common soldiers and sailors. Lenin very cleverly maneuvered himself and the Bolsheviks into a position, in which he could claim that only his party was the real ally of the workers and the men who fought at the front. Combined with Lenin's ongoing demands for an end to the war and for the institution of socialist labor and land policies, Order No. 1 cast the Bolsheviks in the role of promoters of the popular will. For the time being, Kerensky held the reins of the Russian state, but the moment in which the Bolsheviks could seize this power from him was fast approaching. Whether or not Lenin's Bolshevik Party could take advantage of that moment remained to be seen.

Rehearsal for Revolution

LENIN RETURNS

Soon after the Provisional Government replaced Tsar Nicholas II in 1917, a *New York Times* editorial captured the Russian hope for change. Commenting on the political quality of Kerensky and other new leaders of post-tsarist Russia, the newspaper claimed: "Nowhere in their country could the Russian people have found better men to lead them out of the darkness of tyranny."[1] Many in Petrograd that stormy spring would have agreed, but not the city's Bolsheviks. Their leader remained in Switzerland, far from the tumult that accompanied the downfall of the tsar. Lenin was unable to return home for a very simple reason: Between him and Russia lay a vast expanse of German-occupied territory. Much as he would have liked, Lenin could not magically erase the lines drawn on Eastern Europe's map by the victorious German Army and travel openly to Russia. That was, of course, unless the Germans themselves chose to allow him to cross, and that was precisely what they decided to do. Correctly assessing the military potential in fostering political instability in their foe, the Germans encouraged Lenin to return to Petrograd and offered him the means to get there. The Germans gave Lenin safe passage to Russia, via Finland, in a sealed railway car. In exchange, the Germans asked only that Lenin do what he always had promised—what the Kerensky government had as yet refused to do—namely, withdraw Russia from the war and from its alliance with the West.

It was an irresistible offer. The hated Romanovs were gone, the Provisional Government was weak, and the Bolsheviks' popularity was growing. Shortages of food, fuel, and clothing persisted throughout Russia, while the continuing war generated resentment among workers and soldiers. The 300,000 soldiers of the Petrograd garrison and the 30,000 sailors at Kronstadt feared that the Kerensky regime meant to prolong the fighting at the front. Rumors also circulated insinuating that the Provisional Government planned to reinstitute tsarist forms of military order and discipline in a forlorn attempt to reverse the direction of the war. These men were as receptive to the Bolshevik promise of peace as their counterparts in the factories and field were to Bolshevik slogans about worker-controlled industry and land reform. Indeed, driven by guarantees of peace, land, and bread, members swelled the ranks of the Bolshevik Party from 2,000 in early February to more than 16,000 in April. By June, Bolshevik membership would double to 32,000.

Lenin, therefore, brimmed with optimism when he finally returned to Petrograd in April 1917. He was further encouraged by the large and boisterous crowd of Bolshevik faithful who turned out to greet his train at the Finland Station. Lenin took particular notice of the many soldiers, sailors, and non-

Vladimir Lenin, the principal Bolshevik leader of the 1917 Russian Revolution and the first head of the Soviet Union, poses in his study at the Kremlin in October 1918.

Bolsheviks in attendance. Their presence meant that they were prepared to listen seriously to his message, if not ready to join his party at that very moment.

Upbeat and confident, Lenin went to work within hours of his arrival. His first task was to put together an armed wing of the party, a revolutionary strike force called the Bolshevik Military Organization. These fighters would be his vanguard when the time came to employ the violent measures Lenin felt were necessary for a true and lasting socialist revolution. Next, Lenin outlined the party's revised program for Russia's future to receptive minds among the people and the Soviet. Called the April Theses (after the month in which they were released), Lenin's plans and demands were published in *Pravda*. The Bolsheviks called for an immediate transition to a socialist government, an end to the war, government ownership of all factories and banks, ethnic self-determination in Russia's many regions, rural land reform up to and including the redistribution of land from its owners to the peasantry, and the active fomenting of global revolution. Lenin, in short, sought to bring Russia into "the second [Marxist] stage, which should give power into the hands of the proletariat and the poorest strata of the peasantry" without the intervening period of bourgeois capitalist maturation Marx had claimed was crucial to the proper historical setting for revolution.[2] At a subsequent party meeting soon after the April Theses were published, Lenin persuaded the Bolshevik leadership to publicly demand that the Provisional Government transfer its authority and functions to the Petrograd Soviet.

Lenin thus crystallized the Bolshevik goals for anyone still doubting that he viewed 1917 as the year in which the party, with the Soviet as its ally, would ascend to power. The Bolshevik Party, Lenin declared, was to focus its considerable energies on "building up the class consciousness of the proletariat [and] mobilizing it into opposition to the wavering policies of the petty bourgeoisie."[3] Toward that end, he urged a concentration on "increasing and consolidating Bolshevik strength in the soviets."[4] Here he aimed at not only insinuating his party into the Petrograd and Moscow soviets but also into the smaller regional and local ones across Russia. The starting point for all this revolutionary action, Lenin announced, would be the proposed First All-Russian Congress of Soviets of Workers' and Soldiers' Deputies, scheduled to be held in Petrograd in June. At that meeting, the Bolsheviks would move decisively to establish the political preconditions for their seizure of power.

THE PROVISIONAL GOVERNMENT'S WAR

By the spring of 1917, the European powers were mired in a bloody and savage war of attrition all along the Western Front. The Allies and Germans had dug thousands of miles of trenches, from the English Channel to the Swiss border, and from them they slaughtered one another in successive waves of attacks and counterattacks that moved the frontline only a matter of yards. The American entry into the war in April was a ray of hope for the exhausted British and French, to be sure, but no one yet knew whether American troops would arrive at the front soon enough and in sufficient numbers to make a real difference in the fighting. Similarly, the Alpine theater of operations, where the Italians and the Austro-Hungarians were engaged in their own bloodletting, had bogged down. Only in the east did the contending armies still move, and for the Russians it was relentlessly backward. The constant stream of defeats continued after the February Revolution. And, as had been the case under the tsar, the Russian government poured men and matériel into the fight, worsening the economic problems and further lowering morale at home. The net effect was to prevent any real political progress under the new leadership and to open the public's ears ever wider to receive the Bolshevik message.

In May, Kerensky took over the managing of Russia's failing military effort. His appointment as minister of war did nothing to improve matters on the battlefield, but it did identify the SRs and Mensheviks with an unpopular war that the Bolsheviks had sworn to end. Knowing this, Kerensky had two options available to him. One, he could out-Bolshevik the Bolsheviks by suing for peace immediately. Two, Kerensky could gamble on one last attempt to defeat the Germans—one last offensive. The war minister chose the latter. Victory against the Germans in the summer of 1917 would discredit the Bolsheviks and cripple the Petrograd Soviet. Defeat would surely bring down the Provisional Government, inaugurate Bolshevik rule, and create a Soviet Russia.

THE JULY RISING

The Congress of Soviets convened as Russia's generals prepared for the spring offensive. Lenin and the Bolsheviks had long signaled their intention to replace the current leadership of the Petrograd Soviet with Bolsheviks. The Mensheviks, SRs, and others who opposed the Bolsheviks found this notion ludicrous. The Mensheviks, in particular, bristled at the idea—their party had brought down the Romanovs and had successfully constructed a coalition government that included socialists, moderate reformers, and even so-called Kadets, members of the centrist Constitutional Democratic Party. The Bolsheviks, it was said, had done nothing but make speeches, craft slogans, and stir up trouble. As one Menshevik representative to the Congress put it in a speech to the assembly, "[A]t the present moment there is no political party which would say, 'Give the power into our hands, go away, we will take your place.'"[5] A statement to which Lenin responded calmly, "There is."[6] The Bolsheviks did indeed offer an alternative, but it was one not yet welcomed by many Russians. Lenin had been struggling since April to convince the people to accept his party as their best hope for the future, but large segments of the population remained unmoved. So burdened by the weight of leadership, Lenin took a much-needed vacation on the advice of his colleagues. A short time later, Lenin left with his sister for a peaceful cottage in Finland.

Skepticism about the need for radical action, along the lines of that proposed by the Bolsheviks, lingered throughout the spring. It dissipated only with the opening of the July offensive on which Kerensky had wagered his political fortunes. The combined Russian armies under the command of generals Aleksei Brusilov and Lavr Kornilov struck the German and Austrian lines on July 1. Hopes were high within the general staff that this offensive would prove more successful than previous ones and that it could perhaps even turn the tide of war in Russia's favor. Within a few days, however, defeat seemed certain. The Russian advance stopped and then wavered. A swift German counterattack was all it took to break it altogether. From there, the retreat began. A report from the front summed up the situation by saying simply that the Brusilov-Kornilov campaign was "developing into an unprecedented disaster. . . . Most units are in a state of rapidly spreading disintegration."[7]

Worsening food and fuel shortages in Russia only served to highlight the utter collapse of the Russian offensive. The public mood quickly darkened, and people took to the streets. Violent demonstrations broke out in Petrograd on July 4, organized at least in part by the Bolsheviks, without Lenin's permission. Enjoying his rest in Finland, Lenin had been informed neither of the street action in the capital nor of his cadres' role in it. He would learn of these matters after the July Rising had failed. Lacking proper guidance and preparation, the Bolsheviks' efforts, which might have developed into a revolution, instead degenerated into a series of aimless riots that soon spent their energy. The majority of workers and soldiers in the capital sympathized with the July demonstrators, but most of them wanted nothing to do with violence that had no clear political point to it. The July Rising, as a result, was suppressed within a day. The Bolsheviks had moved prematurely, and the outcome had been precisely what Lenin had predicted. Worse yet, the Provisional Government used the July Rising as an excuse to paint the Bolsheviks as dangerous provocateurs and traitors.

"The Bolsheviks are openly acting contrary to the will of the revolutionary democracy," one Petrograd newspaper roared in its front-page denunciation of their July actions.[8] Other newspapers followed suit. Editorial after editorial attacked the Bolsheviks' tactics and motives. One, which appeared a week after the July Rising, even suggested that the demonstrations might have been part of a German plot. The newspaper argued that "the riots cannot be treated as if they were merely the regrettable result of tactical confusion. . . . [They] were an integral part of a plan formulated by the [Germans] to destroy Russia."[9] Another editorial went further and claimed that the Bolshevik Party was itself shot through with traitors and enemy agents. "Among the Bolsheviks," it asserted confidently, "provocateurs and German agents have played and continue to play a great role."[10]

Lenin, upon learning of the uprising and the press's reactions, immediately left for Petrograd. Once back in the capital, he gathered together those responsible for the demonstrations and angrily berated them. They had acted without his knowledge and had jeopardized everything he had worked for. "You should be thrashed for this!" Lenin bellowed.[11] The Bolshevik leader had no time for further criticism, however. He and his party had to brace themselves for the inevitable response of an emboldened Provisional Government and an angry public.

REPRESSION AND EXILE

By the summer of 1917, the Russian people, proletariat and bourgeoisie alike, were clearly disillusioned. Average Russians knew that their country was losing a detested war. The Provisional Government was incompetent, the economy nearly shattered. Nevertheless, Russians retained a powerful attachment to their country. However much Russia might be in desperate need of reform, the patriotism of Russians flourished. Lenin's opponents—chiefly the Kadets, Mensheviks, and SRs—played on this bond between people and place by portraying themselves as agents of change who nonetheless loved their country. Simultaneously, they contrasted their efforts with those of the Bolsheviks. Whereas the Kadets, Mensheviks, and SRs had operated within the Russian mainstream, or so they claimed, the Bolsheviks had gone well beyond what could be tolerated. Yes, they promised change, the Bolsheviks' enemies said, but through violence and collusion with the Germans—that was pure treason.

Isolated and suspect in the eyes of the public, the Bolsheviks were subjected to a campaign of vilification and state-sponsored repression. With increasing harshness, the Bolsheviks were accused of creating disorder and instability in Russia. They were blamed for the failure of the Brusilov offensive; rumors began

STATE AND REVOLUTION

Never content with an idle life, Lenin spent his days in Finland hammering out a new Bolshevik platform based on his ideology of violent revolution. In **State and Revolution** (1917), Lenin laid out a precise set of guidelines for bringing about the advent of a socialist government in Russia and socialist revolution around the world. In the following excerpt, Lenin describes the popular justice and democracy that characterized the socialist interlude that Marx theorized would precede the dawn of Communism:

> From the moment when all members of society, or even only the overwhelming majority, have learned how to govern the state **themselves**, have taken this business into their own hands, have "established" control over the insignificant minority of capitalists, over the gentry with capitalist leanings, and the workers thoroughly demoralized by capitalism—from this moment the need for any government begins

to circulate saying that the Bolsheviks were German saboteurs and paid operatives. The Germans, it was said, had hired Lenin to betray Russia and that German gold in Swiss banks financed Bolshevik activities. A respected Petrograd newspaper even went so far as to suggest a Bolshevik–Black Hundred conspiracy. "It Is Proved," a headline declared, "the Leninists Organized the Uprising in Association with the Black Hundreds!"[12] The fear of Bolshevik treason, however ridiculous, was a boon to the Provisional Government, and to Kerensky in particular. It was on the crest of such delusions that Kerensky rode to his appointment as the Russian prime minister on July 7. Accepting the office without hesitation, Kerensky promised that his administration would "save Russia . . . with blood and iron."[13]

---

to disappear. The more complete the democracy, the nearer the moment when it begins to be unnecessary. The more democratic the "state" consisting of armed workers, which is "no longer a state in a proper sense of the word," the more rapidly does **every** state begin to wither away. For when **all** have learned to manage, and independently are actually managing by themselves social production, keeping accounts, controlling the idlers, the gentlefolk, the swindlers, and similar "guardians of capitalist traditions," then the escape from this national accounting and control will inevitably become so increasingly difficult, such a rare exception, and will probably be accompanied by such swift and severe punishment . . . that very soon the **necessity** of observing the simple, fundamental rules of every-day social life in common will have become a **habit**. The door will then be wide open for the transition from the first phase of Communist society to its higher phase, and along with it to the complete withering away of the state.*

*Vladimir I. Lenin, **State and Revolution**, 1917. New York: International Publishers; reprint 1988, pp. 84-85.

Targeted by both the press and Kerensky, the Bolsheviks soon were being attacked on the streets by ordinary people enflamed by the hysterical rhetoric of their leaders. One government report on anti-Bolshevik violence noted that men "who look like workers or who are suspected of being Bolsheviks are in constant danger of being beaten."[14] According to one Bolshevik sailor, as he and his comrades were returning to their base, they were set upon by a mob "determined to kill us. Some of the attackers said . . . that we were German agents."[15] Kerensky's government nurtured such misrepresentations at every turn and tacitly condoned assaults on Bolsheviks. The Provisional Government took its campaign against the Bolsheviks to the extreme by playing to the virulent anti-Semitism that was commonplace in early twentieth-century Russia. Kerensky's supporters fostered hateful claims that the Bolshevik Party was in truth part of a Jewish group and that "all the blame for the calamities being endured by the country" could be hung on the shoulders of Jewish Bolsheviks.[16]

As prime minister, Kerensky moved with astonishing speed to eliminate the Bolsheviks while they were at their weakest. He ordered the confiscation of privately owned firearms and the disbanding of armed factions such as the Bolshevik Military Organization. Bolshevik newspapers were closed, and the party's headquarters were ransacked. Soldiers' and sailors' committees were broken up, and harsh forms of military discipline were reinstated. The Provisional Government ordered the arrests of Bolshevik leaders Lenin, Lev Kamenev, Grigorii Zinoviev, and Leon Trotsky. Lenin and Zinoviev went into hiding to avoid capture, first at Lenin's sister's house and then once more in Finland. This time, though, Lenin entered Finnish exile with a price on his head. Commenting to a staff worker before leaving Russia, Lenin explained his decision to go: "You, comrade . . . they might arrest. But me, they will hang."[17] Sitting in a tiny straw hut on the shores of a secluded Finnish lake,

Lenin received news of Kamenev's arrest. Trotsky was apprehended and imprisoned on July 23.

By August 1917, the state authorities were dismantling the Bolshevik Party. Its members were frightened; its leadership was in disarray. The leaders remaining in Petrograd—Joseph Stalin, Nikolai Bukharin, and Felix Dzerzhinsky—presided over a political movement teetering on the edge of extinction. One newspaper was so certain of the party's imminent demise that its editors wrote an obituary for it: "The Bolsheviks are compromised, discredited, and crushed. More than that, they have been expelled from Russian life; their teaching has turned out to be an inevitable failure." Or, as a Kadet columnist put it, "Bolshevism has died a sudden death."[18]

And so it might have been, had Lenin not used his time in exile to reorganize the party yet again and redefine its mission. In his hut, Lenin wrote a new party program and a book, *State and Revolution*, to explain it to the masses. Put simply, Lenin refused to lose. Ironically, Kerensky, on the other hand, seemed to refuse to win. Flush with power, Kerensky and his Provisional Government embarked on a crusade to snuff out not only the Bolshevik flame but also the larger fire of continued revolution. The government sought to remove all opposition to its policies, whether in the factories, the military, or the soviets. In this, the state's ambition overreached. It would prove a fatal error.

Resurgence

THE BOLSHEVIKS REBORN

Leon Trotsky was by no means an "old" Bolshevik, having only recently joined the party, but he possessed both a fierce devotion to the cause of global revolution and an abiding loyalty to Lenin. Described at the time as "a fine figure of a man, broadchested, [with] very black hair and goatee beard," Trotsky fought for the party despite his confinement in a prison cell.[1] To those who claimed that the Bolsheviks threatened to roll back the gains of the February Revolution, Trotsky replied, "Lenin has been struggling for the revolution for thirty years. I have been fighting against the oppression of the popular masses for twenty years." Anyone who sought to portray the Bolsheviks as traitors to the revolution or to Russia, according to Trotsky, "does not know what a revolutionary is."[2]

Lenin, in exile in Finland in July 1917, was similarly defiant. The Kerensky government had emerged as the Bolsheviks' nemesis, he contended, but the Petrograd Soviet and its regional counterparts bore the real blame for the repression sweeping Russia and weighing ever more heavily on the Bolshevik Party. "The people must be told the whole truth," Lenin wrote in a letter to the Central Committee. "The present soviets have failed."[3] The only course of action available from this point onward was for the Bolsheviks to rebound and position themselves to take power at the earliest possible opportunity.

While Lenin struggled to endure his exile, the mood in Russia was rapidly shifting. Kerensky's arbitrary arrests and open persecution of the Bolsheviks came against a backdrop of continued military setbacks, economic ruin, critical shortages of basic necessities in the cities, and broken promises of land reform in the countryside. Because the government failed to redistribute land to the people who worked it, 481 peasant uprisings occurred in 1917 alone. Deteriorating factory conditions provoked a new wave of strikes, while the imposition of harsh discipline within the ranks prompted discontent and renewed radicalism among soldiers and sailors. In short, by early August 1917, average Russians were willing to listen to the Bolsheviks again.

Lenin could only be heartened by the news of the renewed interest in his party's ideas, if not yet in its explicit programs. From the regional soviets, the word was even better. Many had openly broken with the larger Petrograd and Moscow soviets over the issue of continued support for Kerensky and had begun to welcome Bolsheviks within their ranks. The Petrograd Soviet itself was rethinking its relationship with the Provisional Government but had not yet embraced the Bolsheviks as an alternative. Mensheviks and SRs maintained a good deal of influence in the Soviet despite their association with Kerensky's failed policies. The result was a cool silence in

Pictured, General Lavr Kornilov inspecting Russian troops in July 1917. Best known today for the Kornilov Affair, an unsuccessful military coup he staged against Kerensky's Provisional Government during the 1917 Russian Revolution, he escaped from prison but was killed fighting the Bolsheviks in the Russian Civil War.

communications among the Petrograd Soviet and its satellites beyond the capital.

Frustrated by such obvious disarray and bickering, the Bolsheviks decided to push forward independently until they were in a position to exercise more power in the Petrograd Soviet and in regional soviets. They thus sought to bring down the government while simultaneously maneuvering to gain a commanding role in the soviets. The first step in both directions was participation in the August Petrograd city duma elections. The Bolshevik showing in the balloting, coming as it did on the heels of the government's efforts to break the party, was nothing less than astonishing. Bolshevik candidates won 67 seats in the Duma, second only to the radical faction of the SRs, which took 75. The conservative Kadets netted 42 seats; the Mensheviks came in at an embarrassing 8 seats total. Such a positive result encouraged Lenin to keep up the political pressure and to work more closely with Stalin, the manager of the party in its leader's absence. Together they decided that the Duma elections had given the party a new respectability and that there would be no better time to win over the Petrograd Soviet.

KORNILOV'S REVOLT

This would indeed prove to be the best moment for a move against the Provisional Government. Even before the Duma elections, developments within the ruling elite were conspiring to give the Bolsheviks an opening to power. Of the many obstacles the Bolsheviks faced in their resurgence, conservative army officers represented perhaps the greatest. The upper echelons of the Russian Army had opposed the February Revolution and the establishment of the Provisional Government, but the generals had tolerated it nonetheless. Kerensky had continued the war and had put the disciplinary leash back around the necks of ordinary soldiers and sailors. The Provisional Government, moreover, had signaled its willingness to collaborate with conservative political groups, the Orthodox Church, and the industrial bourgeoisie to maintain Russia's class system and traditions. From the military's point of view, Kerensky was certainly not the tsar, but neither was he Lenin; and the Mensheviks posed little threat to the traditions the officer corps prized above all else. Still, the Provisional Government had angered many top generals by seeming irresolute in war and unreliable in dealing with the Bolsheviks. Along with several influential Kadet politicians and diehard monarchists, the generals began to consider the possibility of replacing Kerensky with one of their own. Thoughts of a military coup arose.

If the army took power, there were many candidates available for consideration for the job of military dictator. The list included General Aleksei Brusilov, Admiral Aleksandr Kolchak, General Mikhail Alekseyev, and General Lavr Kornilov. Of these men, Kornilov was the most likely choice to succeed Kerensky. Privately described by his peers as an "absolute ignoramus in the realm of politics" and "a man with a lion's heart and the brains of a sheep,"[4] Kornilov was a violent antisocialist who despised the Provisional Government just slightly less than he hated the Bolsheviks. More so than the others, Kornilov would greet the chance to engineer Kerensky's downfall with unrestrained glee. The general, in fact, already had bullied Kerensky into making him the Russian Army's commander in chief and recently had submitted a list of military demands to the government that included military control of Russia's railroads and war industries. An overt challenge to Kerensky at this point would surprise no one.

Kerensky had long suspected Kornilov of harboring political ambitions. On August 3, he requested a face-to-face meeting with the general, a conference that quickly degenerated into a shouting match. Kerensky was furious that Kornilov's machine-gun company had taken up positions around the Winter Palace prior to the meeting. Kornilov accused Kerensky of disregarding the needs of the military.

Three days later, Kornilov quietly rearranged his troops around Petrograd and made the final decision to move against the Provisional Government. He acted on August 19. Citing intelligence reports that indicated an imminent Bolshevik uprising, Kornilov put the units of the Petrograd Military District under his command. It was "high time," Kornilov exclaimed, "to hang the German agents and spies headed by Lenin . . . [and] hang the entire Soviet membership."[5] Within a week, Kornilov put the capital under martial law and ordered his army stationed nearby to enter the city. The coup had begun.

Kerensky's first step in defense of his government was to relieve Kornilov of his command. Kornilov's refusal to step down and the proximity of his army sent the Provisional Government into a blind panic. Frantically, the ministers turned to the Petrograd Soviet and pleaded for an alliance. The Soviet, having been identified as a Bolshevik appendage and targeted for destruction by Kornilov, readily agreed. Together, the Soviet and the government formed the Committee for the Struggle Against the Counterrevolution. Kerensky was relieved until he learned of the Soviet's only condition in establishing the committee—armed Bolshevik participation.

Although the Soviet was openly accepting a commanding Bolshevik presence, Lenin, still in Finland, astounded his comrades in Petrograd by instructing them to reject the offer. He feared that Kerensky and Kornilov had concocted a sham crisis in order to lure the Bolsheviks into premature action. Lenin felt that the entire idea of an alliance was a trap set for his party by those seeking its destruction. Stalin and the others in Petrograd saw it differently and offered to provide the Soviet and the government with armed workers, or Bolshevik Red Guards, to lead the fight against Kornilov. They also quietly ordered Bolshevik cadres within the Petrograd garrison to begin agitating for a wholesale defection from Kornilov's command to the Committee and the Red Guard. Their work produced

A photo of Red Guards firing from an armored vehicle in Moscow, during the 1917 Russian Revolution.

quick and positive results. With only a very few exceptions, the garrison swung behind the government coalition, as did over 30,000 sailors from Kronstadt. Along with the Red Guards, the soldiers and sailors moved out into the streets of the capital to defend key government buildings, strategic bridges, and vital communication centers. In the waters offshore, Bolshevik-led sailors even seized a number of warships and ran up red banners to proclaim their loyalties.

As Petrograd's defense grew more formidable, Kornilov's revolt began to unravel. His units started to defect to the Red Guards en masse, with officers increasingly following their men in doing so. Sensing that Kornilov was becoming a liability, many of his fellow generals distanced themselves from the reactionary figure whose star was now quite obviously falling. Kornilov, by August 30, was a commander without an army and a conspirator without a plot. The general soon was arrested and replaced as commander in chief by General Alekseyev. The

Provisional Government had been saved, but only through the efforts of the Bolshevik Party. Kerensky sheepishly acknowledged as much and ordered the release of all Bolshevik prisoners still being held since the July arrests, including Trotsky. Kornilov's revolt elevated the Bolsheviks into the ranks of national saviors.

DECISION ON THE LEFT

The fallout from the Kornilov Affair spread across the political spectrum, beginning on the right. Kadets, in and out of government, pressed Kerensky to leave office and accept Alekseyev as his replacement. British and other Western diplomats in Petrograd urged the prime minister to negotiate a power-sharing deal with the general staff and to squash the Bolshevik movement. Mensheviks and SRs called for significant reforms and the suppression of both the Bolsheviks and the counterrevolutionary elements within the army. At the other end, the Bolsheviks were united in opposition to Kerensky's government but divided on the issue of compromise with other socialists. Some Bolsheviks thought it might be best to cooperate with radical Mensheviks and SRs, at least for the moment. Others, such as the Red Guards, soldiers, and sailors, demanded the removal of Kerensky, an end to conservative influence in state administration, and the immediate transfer of power to the soviets. On this count, those Bolsheviks who rejected the notion of cooperation with other elements had the support of many factory workers who argued that "power must not remain in the hands of the counterrevolutionary bourgeoisie a minute longer. It must be put into the hands of the workers, soldiers, and poorer peasantry."[6] A widely read newspaper agreed. The Russian people, its editors wrote, "have had quite enough compromise! All power to the working people."[7]

Bolstered by such sentiments, Lenin commanded the Central Committee in September to submit a resolution to the Soviet that called for transferring state authority to

organs of the working class, as well as the immediate sever-
ing of any connections with the Mensheviks and Kadets. To
even Lenin's surprise, the Soviet approved the resolution—all
power would go to the soviets and no compromise would be
made with centrists and conservatives. Yet as soon as he had
won this victory, Lenin then reversed himself and recom-
mended compromise with sympathetic leftwing Mensheviks
and SRs. Bolsheviks in the Soviet were shocked by this abrupt
about-face, but they complied.

On September 7, the Soviet reorganized its top administrative offices to provide for a committee made up of
four Bolsheviks, two SRs, and one Menshevik; Trotsky was

ALL POWER TO THE SOVIETS!

The Bolshevik relationship with the Petrograd Soviet was
often stormy, due in large part to the great numbers of
Menshevik and SR deputies who held seats in it. The call,
therefore, to transfer state authority to the Soviet was not
one Lenin embraced until it became clear that he and his
party could use the Soviet to accomplish their ends. By
September 1917, Lenin was quite comfortable in demanding that power be transferred to the Soviet's deputies, but
his earlier opposition still had to be rationalized. This Lenin
did by simply redefining what the phrase "All Power to the
Soviets!" meant:

> The slogan "Power to the Soviets" is very often incorrectly
> interpreted to mean "a cabinet of the parties of the Soviet
> majority." . . . "Power to the Soviets" means radically reshap-
> ing the entire old state apparatus, that bureaucratic apparatus

selected as its chairman. Taking the compromise model further, the Soviet convened a Democratic State Conference in the capital on September 14 to discuss Russia's future. A mix of political operatives, trade unionists, and local officials, the conference members listened as Bolshevik representatives advised that a coalition of socialist groups, via the soviets, assume control of the state. Trotsky even revived the old slogan "All Power to the Soviets!" Unity was the keyword at the State Conference.

Then, without warning, Lenin inexplicably changed his mind once again and rejected all forms of collaboration. Furthermore, he told the party to prepare an imminent armed

which hampers everything democratic. It means removing this apparatus and substituting for it a new popular one, i.e., a truly democratic apparatus of soviets, i.e., the organized and armed majority of the people—the workers, soldiers, and peasants. It means allowing the majority of the people initiative and independence not only in the election of deputies, but also in state administration, in effecting reforms and various other changes.*

By altering perhaps the most recognizable political slogan in Russia to mean erecting a new revolutionary order rather than reinforcing the current one, Lenin could claim to support the Soviet while undercutting his Menshevik and SR opponents. Any transfer of government power to the Soviet, therefore, would necessarily be a shift favorable to the Bolsheviks.

*Alexander Rabinowitch, **The Bolsheviks Come to Power: The Revolution of 1917 in Petrograd.** Chicago, Ill. and Ann Arbor, Mich.: Haymarket Books and Pluto Press, 2004, p. 171.

insurrection. His confused comrades in Petrograd reacted coolly. An armed insurrection now, they reasoned, might actually strengthen Kerensky and the Provisional Government and paint the Bolshevik Party as a threat to national security, as had happened in July. The Germans, meanwhile, were advancing into Russian territory. A Bolshevik uprising could prompt Kerensky to surrender in return for German assistance in eradicating Bolshevism. Lenin was deaf to such rationale. From Finland, he sent a series of telegrams to the Central Committee ordering it to begin an armed assault on the government. He stridently asserted that Mensheviks and SRs were not worthy of cooperation because, as he wrote in his book *State and Revolution*, they were not true socialists at all, but rather "petty-bourgeois democrats with a near-Socialist phraseology."[8]

Finland, however, was not Petrograd. Lounging at his lakeside hut, Lenin could easily talk of armed insurrection and the immediate seizure of state authority. But the situation in the capital was more delicate. The Bolsheviks there had to move cautiously, if they were not to overplay their hand. Trotsky, Bukharin, and Stalin all agreed that it was better to wait for political matters to develop a bit further before taking action. The Central Committee voted unanimously to ignore any further instructions from Lenin. When the time was right, as they saw it, Trotsky and the others would initiate a Bolshevik revolution, and not before, regardless of Lenin's wishes.

Lenin, failing to receive any response to his telegrams, accurately deduced what was happening. He was losing control of the party he had created almost 25 years earlier. The Bolshevik movement he had painstakingly crafted through years of disappointment, exile, and imprisonment was slipping away from him. If Lenin did not return to Petrograd, he risked becoming utterly irrelevant. Shaving his trademark goatee and donning a wig to cover his famously bald head, Lenin left Finland on September 17, 1917. He was bound for the capital—and for a revolution.

October Days

LENIN RETURNS—AGAIN

Lenin feared that both the Bolshevik Party and its best chance for a Bolshevik revolution were drifting beyond his control. Party leaders in Petrograd had ignored his wishes, even while the masses were eager for any kind of change. Lenin worried that his movement might lose its popular base of support if the workers, soldiers, and sailors moved toward other leftist political groups. He had to act; he had to return to Russia and reassert his authority. Only then could he place the Bolsheviks in a position to exploit the post-Kornilov reaction and to seize the state from the hands of an increasingly feeble Provisional Government.

   This would not be the first time the Bolshevik leader had come home from exile. Cheering crowds and red banners had greeted him upon his arrival in April, but as he stepped off the train in September 1917, all he encountered was the evidence of a nation in despair. Petrograd, a city of 2.7 million people, was sliding into utter chaos. After the aborted Kornilov coup, the Kerensky government was quickly losing what little popular credibility it had left. The Mensheviks, as a party, were following Kerensky into public disfavor and oblivion; the Socialist Revolutionaries had been frozen by indecision for months and no longer acted like either socialists or revolutionaries. The economy was disintegrating, and Russia clearly had lost the war.

Only the Bolsheviks could offer any genuine hope of rescue, but they were locked in the bitter dispute over the next step to take on the road to power. Some in the party preached the virtues of compromise with Mensheviks and SRs, who now had no option but to deal with their old enemy; others advocated confrontation, a swift and violent settling of accounts with the Provisional Government and its supporters. Both sides, however, agreed on one thing: now was not the time for action. An uprising at that very moment would be not only foolhardy but premature. The quarreling Bolsheviks also agreed that the next move, whatever it might be, had to be decided at the All-Russian Congress of Soviets, originally set to convene on October 20 and later postponed until October 25. Any action taken prior to the Congress might look like a betrayal of the popular trust and could cost the Bolsheviks the strong support they had gained in the soviets. Leaving matters to the Congress of Soviets suited both the party's collaborationists, such as Kamenev, and the oppositionists, like Trotsky. Bolsheviks, they reasoned, already controlled the committee of the Petrograd Soviet, and the Bolshevik delegation certainly would be capable of dominating and directing the Congress. It was agreed, then, to wait until October 25. After that, the revolution would come.

Lenin, confounded and angry, threatened to resign. If the party would not obey him, then there was no point in his continuing in its leadership. At this point, fate intervened on Lenin's behalf. The telegrams he had written urging immediate armed revolt, the ones the Central Committee chose to ignore, were leaked to the public. Within hours, the Petrograd and Moscow soviets broke with the Central Committee over what was perceived to be the latter's betrayal of its own founder and his principles. Both bodies quickly announced their open support for Lenin and Trotsky. Two days after the telegrams appeared and the Soviets swung behind Lenin, Trotsky returned the favor. At the October 7 opening of the Provisional Government's new session at the Mariinsky Palace, Trotsky disrupted the proceedings with an impromptu speech in which he labeled Kerensky a traitor. "The revolution and the people are in danger!" Trotsky called out over a shocked assembly. "We turn to the people! All power to the soviets!"[1] He then turned and stormed out.

THE TURNING POINT

On the evening of October 10, Lenin secretly met with the members of the Central Committee in a small Petrograd apartment. Still in disguise, Lenin faced off against his opponents on the issue of violent revolution. Trotsky pledged to back his leader; Stalin did likewise, if only to enhance his standing in the Bolshevik hierarchy. Kamenev and Zinoviev, who persisted in their opposition to both an immediate uprising and to violence in general, counseled patience and cooperation to effect a bloodless takeover of the Russian government. Lenin, though, was adamant. The time for revolution had arrived, he contended, and violence was an absolute necessity if that revolution were to be secured. Lenin added that the masses were now prepared to follow the Bolsheviks, but this might not always be the case.

Days passed before Lenin persuaded the Central Committee that the moment had come to bring down the Provisional

Pictured, a large crowd assembled in Red Square, with Bolshevik leaders Joseph Stalin (*right*) and Leon Trotsky standing on a podium, during the 1917 Russian Revolution.

Government. Soon afterward, the Committee issued an order to the party cadres calling for armed insurrection. The only condition attached to the order was that any uprising be portrayed as a defense of the Soviet against Kerensky. People had to think that if the Bolsheviks seized power, as Lenin prescribed, "we seize it not against the soviets but for them."[2] Even Lenin understood that the soldiers of the Petrograd garrison and the sailors at Kronstadt would aid the Bolsheviks only if convinced that the party was acting on behalf of the Soviet, to which they already had given their loyalty. Receiving the Central Committee's directive, Bolshevik operatives throughout the capital swung into action.

Moderates and conservatives in Petrograd sensed that the Bolsheviks were up to something. Most agreed that, as a Kadet newspaper put it, "the vile and bloody events of July 3–5 were only a rehearsal. Now the Bolsheviks are preparing to give the performance itself."[3] That performance would most likely be accompanied by a symphony of gunfire. Kerensky, resting uneasily in the Winter Palace, knew that restraint at this point would be an invitation to his own ouster. He could not afford to aid the Bolsheviks through indecision. The prime minister also understood that the Petrograd garrison had been thoroughly infiltrated by Bolshevik cadres. He had to move against it first before turning to the Bolsheviks themselves.

His plan involved great risks. Kerensky had to find a way to redeploy the Petrograd troops and replace them with ones loyal to the Provisional Government. The first step would be the quiet removal of Bolshevik agitators and organizers from the ranks, followed by the reassignment of the units they had corrupted with their talk of a Bolshevik revolution. Next, the rest of the city's garrison would be moved out of the capital, unit by unit. New soldiers from the front would be brought in, and Kerensky would use those troops to smash the Bolsheviks and their entire apparatus once and for all.

Never famous for his stealth, Kerensky revealed himself to be dangerously clumsy during these crucial days in October 1917. The Petrograd Soviet saw through his scheme almost from the moment Kerensky began its implementation. Everyone recognized that Kerensky was trying to monopolize the available armed forces in preparation of the dissolution of the Soviet and the arrest of its members. Fearful for its very existence, the Soviet turned to the Bolsheviks for protection and formed a joint defense force built around the Bolshevik

Military Organization; it was called the Military Revolutionary Committee (MRC) and was tasked with preserving the security and authority of the Soviet. Should Kerensky succeed in redeploying the sympathetic garrison, the Bolshevik-led MRC was commanded to resist any effort to disband the Soviet and any attempt at a counterrevolution. Kerensky had unwittingly united his enemies and vastly increased Lenin's influence in the streets.

MOMENTUM BUILDS

Lenin packed the leadership of the MRC with high-ranking Bolsheviks almost as soon as it was formed. He included a few leftwing SRs to give the impression of balance, but Lenin pointedly excluded all Mensheviks from participation. He did not want any interference from Kerensky's followers as he molded the MRC into a Bolshevik army. Once in charge of the committee and its guns, Lenin used the Soviet Day celebrations on October 22 as a cover to act against the government. While Bolshevik speakers addressed crowds throughout the city, Bolshevik soldiers and sailors took on the role of political commissars in the barracks and prepared the troops to act in concert with the MRC. The MRC, meanwhile, sent armed men to occupy the grounds of the Peter and Paul Fortress, an artillery post adjacent to Petrograd's main weapons arsenal that was just within shelling range of the Winter Palace.

On October 24, Kerensky countered Lenin's moves by calling for the arrest of the entire MRC and issuing an official request for troops camped outside Petrograd to advance and take up stations within the city. The Provisional Government stunned Lenin and the Bolshevik leadership with the speed of its response, but the party quickly recovered and announced to its members that "Kerensky is on the offensive . . . the Petrograd Soviet is in direct danger."[4] Trotsky, in command of the MRC, assured Lenin that it was ready for combat if needed.

The tension was building as, yet again, the more timid members of the Central Committee balked. Perhaps, they said, the threat of violence was enough; perhaps Kerensky should be given an opportunity to negotiate. Lenin would have none of it. "Comrades," he stated without hesitation, "it is now absolutely clear that to delay the uprising would be fatal. . . . We must not wait! We may lose everything!"[5] The Provisional Government was at its weakest, Lenin argued, and for that reason it "must be *given the deathblow* at all costs. To delay action is fatal."[6] After some discussion, the Central Committee conceded the point. There would be no more talk of restraint, only of violent revolt.

OCTOBER 25

The Kerensky regime's power was eroding with each passing minute. The prime minister's plea for troops resulted in the mustering of a token force consisting of 2,000 young military cadets and 200 women of the First Petrograd Women's Shock Battalion. The rest of the soldiers either refused to march or, worse, had openly defected to the Bolsheviks and the MRC. Increasingly isolated, Kerensky addressed his government and the Russian people in a rambling speech late on October 24. Obviously nervous, Kerensky declared that the recent Bolshevik actions "constitute treason and a betrayal of the Russian state. . . . Arrests have been ordered," he assured the nation.[7] Kerensky's words did nothing to reduce the tension that filled the autumn air in Petrograd. Reports already were coming in, describing episodes of minor street clashes between forces loyal to the government and those of the Bolshevik Red Guards.

Lenin dismissed Kerensky's speech as the last gasp of a dying political order. He pushed the insurrection into its next phase. The Bolsheviks had no time to waste; they had to complete their takeover of the government before the Congress of Soviets met that day. If Lenin could proclaim his party to be the rulers of Russia at the very beginning of the session, the Congress would

A photo of Bolshevik soldiers protesting in the streets of Petrograd during the revolution.

have little choice but to validate the Bolsheviks' actions. Speed was essential. At 2:00 A.M., Bolshevik-commanded soldiers and Red Guards seized Petrograd's rail stations and main post office. Moments later, Bolsheviks took over the capital's power transfer station and cut electricity to all government offices and the Winter Palace. Over the course of the next few hours, sailors aboard the cruiser *Aurora* maneuvered the ship to a station on the Neva River in front of the palace and then took the bridges linking the government complex to the rest of the city. Red Guards, at 6:00 A.M., stormed into Petrograd's central bank; an hour later, they did likewise at the main telephone exchange and disconnected the telephone lines connecting Kerensky's offices to the army headquarters at Mogilev. Kerensky and his administration were sealed off. Government ministers desperately sought some way to escape from Petrograd; Kerensky already

A REVOLUTION IN THE STREETS

The Provisional Government received little good news on October 25, 1917. Army officers loyal to the Kerensky regime filed one report after another that made clear the dire situation on the streets of Petrograd. The two communications below are typical of those that flooded the main army headquarters on the day the Bolsheviks seized power:

[Early morning wire from Kerensky's aide-de-camp, General Levitsky, to the Russian Army chief of staff, General Dukhonin] Part of the Petrograd garrison . . . joined the Bolsheviks; sailors arrived from Kronstadt. . . . The whole city is covered with [troops], who at present manifest no activity of any kind. The telephone exchange is in the hands of the insurgent troops. . . . One has the feeling that the Provisional Government is in the capital of an enemy which has just completed mobilization but has not yet begun military operations."

[10:15 A.M. direct wire to headquarters by the commander in chief of the Petrograd District, Colonel Polkovnikov] The situation in Petrograd is menacing. There are no street disorders, but a systematic seizure of government buildings and railway stations is going on. None of my orders is obeyed. . . . I must report, conscious of my responsibility to the country, that the Provisional Government is in danger. There is no guaranty [sic] that the insurrectionists will not next attempt to arrest the Provisional Government.*

*James Bunyan and Harold Henry Fisher, **The Bolshevik Revolution, 1917-1918: Documents and Materials**. Stanford, Calif.: Stanford University Press, 1934, pp. 98-99.

had arranged to leave Petrograd, with the help of the American ambassador, should Lenin's uprising prove successful.

Meeting at the MRC headquarters, Lenin, Trotsky, Stalin, and the rest of the Bolshevik leadership began drafting plans for their assumption of power. They first congratulated one another on a job well done and then sat down to discuss the shape of the new Bolshevik government. The group decided to scrap the old ministerial offices and the titles that went along with them in favor of commissariats. Trotsky suggested that top government officials be referred to as "people's commissars," to which Lenin responded happily, "Yes, that's very good; it smells of revolution."[8] The Russian government itself henceforth would be known as *Sovnarkom*—the Council of People's Commissars—and Lenin would be its chief.

THE FINAL ACT

As the Bolsheviks debated proper titles for themselves, revolutionary actions were continuing across the capital and spreading to Moscow and beyond. As Lenin and the others discussed strategy, the Baltic Fleet was mutinying. Bolshevik soldiers occupied the Mariinsky Palace and surrounded the Winter Palace, demanding its surrender under the threat of shelling by the *Aurora*. Kerensky delayed his response in order to finalize his escape plan and begged the American ambassador to help him leave the country. The Americans sent an embassy touring car for the beleaguered prime minister. The car, flying the American flag, arrived at the Winter Palace and promptly whisked Kerensky to safety. He eventually would enter into exile in the United States. Lenin paid little attention to Kerensky's actions; he was too busy drafting a revolutionary proclamation announcing the fall of the Provisional Government and the rise of his own. The collapse of the government, such as it was after Kerensky's departure, came quickly. By the late afternoon of October 25, Trotsky could definitively say to the Soviet that "the Provisional Government no longer exists!"[9] The Bolsheviks had triumphed.

Amid the confusion of the Bolshevik revolution, the Second All-Russian Congress of Soviets convened. Despite the obvious Bolshevik victory that had just taken place, the Menshevik and SR delegates tried frantically to reverse the outcome. The only tool left to them, however, was one Lenin had discredited long before—compromise. Some, disgusted with their colleagues and resigned to defeat, simply walked out rather than beg for Bolshevik good graces. The remaining Mensheviks and SRs took turns appealing to the Bolsheviks' political sensibilities. For Russia's sake, the petitioners asked, could not some kind of arrangement be worked out? Trotsky's blistering reply mocked such presumption:

> With whom ought we to compromise? With those wretched groups who have left us or who are making this proposal? . . . No one in Russia is with them any longer. . . . No, here no compromise is possible. . . . You are miserable bankrupts, your role is played out; go where you ought to go: into the dustbin of history![10]

Denied any hope of participation in the shaping of Russia's political and social future, the defeated Mensheviks and SRs filed out of the Congress. For the rest of the convention, the Congress of Soviets was essentially a Bolshevik Party meeting.

The last holdouts at the Winter Palace, a handful of cold, hungry army cadets, surrendered the grand old building to a detachment of Red Guards at precisely 2:00 A.M. on October 26, 1917. The few government ministers who had stayed behind were arrested. Lenin now could proclaim to the world that a new Bolshevik Russia had been born. As the German socialist Karl Kautsky put it, the Bolsheviks had "made, for the first time in world history, a socialist party the ruler of a great power."[11] Lenin's followers celebrated what they were convinced was the beginning of a global revolution and a new era for humanity. It was, as one local soviet declared, "the beginning of the worldwide commune. We, as the leaders, assume full responsibility and fear nothing."[12] The Bolsheviks did indeed fear nothing in October 1917. However, such assertions, like the Bolshevik Revolution itself, were premature. The enemies of Bolshevism still lived and could yet strike out against Lenin and his newborn Soviet Russia. Indeed, the Bolsheviks had a great deal still to fear.

8

Reds and Whites

THE WHITE FRONT FORMS

The Bolsheviks might have won the day in October 1917, but their revolutionary victory was hardly secure. Powerful enemies remained. Russian armies were still in the field, many commanded by men who loathed the Bolsheviks. Nor was the war with Germany at an end. Lenin, therefore, faced a dual threat. The Bolsheviks would have to make peace with the Germans, something Lenin had long promised the Russian people, before extinguishing the last embers of the old order still smoldering in places such as Siberia and the Ukraine.

Far from the streets of Petrograd and Moscow, powerful antirevolutionary forces had gathered, known collectively as the Whites. The Bolsheviks had hung that name on them in an attempt to identify their foes with the supporters of

King Louis XVI, who had failed in their efforts to destroy the French Revolution in the 1790s. The name also conveniently contrasted with the Bolshevik Reds. In truth, the Whites represented an assemblage of disparate anti-Bolshevik groups ranging from unrepentant Mensheviks and militant SRs to army officers still loyal to the slain tsar. However diverse they were, the Whites shared a hatred of the Bolsheviks and a determination to drive them from power. This singular goal brought the Whites together, in January 1918, around a core of key army officers led by General Alekseyev, General Anton Denikin, and Admiral Kolchak. Coincidentally, as the White front was forming, the Bolsheviks were formalizing their military structure, creating both a Red Army and a Red Fleet to defend the new regime. As the two opposing sides armed against each other, the final phase of the Bolshevik Revolution began: a Russian civil war.

Although strong emotions and ideologies animated both the Whites and the Reds, the Bolsheviks held the upper hand militarily. The Bolsheviks possessed a unified command, managed closely by Lenin and Trotsky, and had the advantage of fighting on the defensive. The Bolsheviks did not have to win; they just had to not lose. Additionally, due to the positions of the opposing armies, the Bolsheviks would operate in a smaller geographic area with interior lines of supply and communication. Red territory, moreover, had a relatively homogeneous, predominantly Russian population of 70 million, many of whom were urbanized and well educated. The Bolsheviks would not have to deal with ethnic rivalries, nor would the Red Army suffer for men. The size and composition of the Soviet population gave the Reds access to a pool of nearly 3 million high-quality recruits.

Adding to these Bolshevik advantages was the availability of weapons and experienced troops held over from the imperial army. Granted, most of the trained soldiers were enlisted men who had only joined the revolution in October, but their morale was strong. Some officers accompanied their troops into Bolshevik service, but the real influx of experienced commanders would come later. Similarly, the Bolsheviks had an arsenal of modern weapons at their disposal, thanks to the tsarist army of 1914–1917, which had stored most of its arms in places now under Bolshevik control. Bolshevik stockpiles in early 1918 amounted to nearly 2.5 million rifles, 1.2 billion rounds of small-arms ammunition, 12,000 artillery pieces, and 28 million artillery shells.

The only significant Bolshevik handicap was the limited supply of grain available to their fighting forces. Russia's agricultural base always had been the Ukraine, a region hostile to the Bolsheviks and currently under the control of Alekseyev and Denikin's Volunteer Army. The vast fields of the Ukraine and those in the parts of Siberia occupied by Kolchak's troops produced more grain than the Whites would ever need. The White armies thus had ready access to food, a fact that might have compensated for the imbalance in men and guns, had other factors not skewed the number yet further in the Bolsheviks' favor.

The Whites were disorganized and had a command system that made joint maneuvers difficult at best. The White base of operation was huge geographically, but it possessed few railroads and only the most primitive highway system. Transport and communication became nagging problems for the Whites in the upcoming struggle. For such a vast space, the population living under White authority was small, dispersed, undereducated, and diverse. From this demographic base, the Whites would never be able to draw more than 250,000 multiethnic peasant soldiers to augment the forces already at hand. These recruits lacked a common language and, in most cases, any military training. They also would have to endure the chronic shortages of arms and ammunition that routinely hampered White operations. The core of the White armies, however, was

White (Imperial) Russian troops march down the street of an occupied city on a recruitment drive. The Whites' unfocused counterrevolutionary efforts led to their eventual defeat by the Bolsheviks during the Russian Civil War.

solid, especially that of the Volunteer Army, built as it was upon the Cossack units from the Don River region. The Cossacks were loyal men with a reputation for skill, ferocity, and devotion to traditional authority. The Whites in the Ukraine also had access to a small, well-trained army under the command of the renegade general Kornilov.

BREST-LITOVSK

As the Whites and Reds prepared to confront each other on the battlefield, Lenin was working feverishly to end the war with Germany. Partly in order to gain some measure of respectability on the world stage, Lenin changed the name of the Bolshevik

Party to the Communist Party of Russia in March 1918. The term *Bolshevik*, he felt, implied revolution; *Communist*, on the other hand, sounded more traditionally Marxist. Bolshevism was Russian, moreover, but Marxism was German in origin and international in its attraction. Germans might relate better to Communists than to Bolsheviks. Either way, Lenin had promised peace, and now he had to deliver. Civil war drew closer every day. For this, if for no other reason, the Bolsheviks had to end the fighting on the Eastern Front.

Lenin's Decree on Peace, issued shortly after the October Revolution, called for an immediate end to hostilities, but it had no real diplomatic value. The decree's intention was "to bring to a successful conclusion the work of peace," but pulling Russia out of World War I would require more than words.[1] A treaty with Germany would have to be negotiated and signed. Negotiations were difficult in the best of times, and now the Bolsheviks would need to sit down at the bargaining table while the White forces were gathering for an offensive. It would not be easy to deal with the Germans under such circumstances. In truth, though, by January 1918, the Russians already had been discussing a peace agreement with the Germans at Brest-Litovsk, in what is today the nation of Belarus. Both governments stood to gain from a negotiated peace. The Bolsheviks could concentrate their resources on defending the revolution, while the Germans could transfer their eastern armies to the Western Front for a planned spring 1918 offensive against the British and French. Trotsky led the Russian delegation and a team of generals headed the German delegation, reflecting the political goals of the Bolsheviks and the military objectives of the Germans.

An armistice came early in January. The Germans and the other Central Powers, by the terms of the agreement, could retain any occupied territory they currently held, in return for a pledge not to transfer combat troops to the West. The Bolsheviks won the right for Russian soldiers to discuss socialist theory with German troops after the armistice went into effect. In this way, Lenin hoped to incite a revolution in the rest of Europe, starting in Germany. The job of explaining to the party how a truce could be arranged with an alliance of capitalist, imperialist monarchies fell to the chief of the Russian negotiating team, Trotsky. He described it as simply a logical first step toward global socialism.

After the initial breakthrough, however, talks aimed at a signed peace treaty first stalled and then broke down altogether. On February 17, frustrated and fearing some sort of Bolshevik trick, the Germans resumed hostilities, which forced Russia's hand. Talks reopened on March 3 and culminated in a formal treaty that allowed Germany to keep all occupied territory and required Russia to drop any financial claims related to the war. The Bolsheviks received little more than the peace they craved from the Treaty of Brest-Litovsk. That was enough, however. As Lenin rationalized, "a disgraceful peace is proper, because it is in the interest of the proletarian revolution and the regeneration of Russia."[2] The treaty ended not only Russia's war but also its alliance with the Western Allies, an outcome that infuriated the British, French, and Americans and uniformly turned them against the Bolshevik regime.

WHITE VICTORIES AND INTERVENTION

Peace with Germany still left the Bolsheviks facing the White generals, who struck first in the spring of 1918. Red outposts and strongholds were attacked along the Siberian and Ukrainian frontiers. When Kornilov was killed by a Bolshevik shell in one of the early battles, Bolsheviks began to falsely hope for a quick end to the fighting. Rather, it intensified and was compounded by the landing of 70,000 Japanese soldiers at the port city of Vladivostok. The Japanese move was the first of many foreign interventions to come in the months ahead.

The Bolsheviks' problems grew in May 1918. During World War I, the imperial army had formed Czech prisoners into a volunteer unit known as the Czech Legion. Expecting to be repatriated after the Treaty of Brest-Litovsk, the Czech soldiers rebelled when it became apparent that the Bolshevik government would let them go home only if they surrendered their weapons. The Legion immediately gained the open approval and support of the Western powers and the White generals. Both saw the Czechs as the leading edge of a new anti-Red coalition. By July, their hopes seemed to be confirmed when the Czechs captured several key Bolshevik towns, including Yekaterinburg. It was the Czechs, in fact, who discovered the first evidence of the Romanov killings.

Through the summer and fall, the news from the fronts was relentlessly bad for the Bolsheviks. The White Volunteer Army in the south won a string of victories and even set up a rival government in the areas it controlled. Then, British intervention forces landed at Murmansk on the Arctic coast. In September, they were joined by the French, who came ashore at Archangel. American troops appeared at both Archangel and Vladivostok. The administration of President Woodrow Wilson stated publicly that "military action is admissible in Russia . . . to steady any efforts at self-government or self-defense" by the Whites.[3] Having already severed relations with the Bolsheviks in December 1917, the United States was prepared to help restore a less-threatening government in Petrograd. Privately, however, President Wilson conceded that "to try to stop a revolutionary movement by a line of armies is to employ a broom to stop a great flood."[4]

The Bolsheviks did what they could to resist the combined White-Czech-Allied forces arrayed against them. Toward the British and American armies, the Bolsheviks cast revolutionary slogans and propaganda in the hopes of eroding support for intervention among the common troops. "You will be fighting not against enemies," the Bolsheviks reminded the Allied soldiers, "but against working people like yourselves. We ask you [as workers], are you going to crush us?"[5] The Bolshevik message of class unity resonated with many men on the other side; morale did decline, but the intervention armies remained in place. In Siberia, following Denikin's lead, Kolchak set up his own government and, like Denikin in the Ukraine, began a program of methodical persecution of Bolsheviks and Jews. The Whites revived the specter of Jewish Bolshevism, claiming that "the present regime is Jewish and therefore also diabolical."[6] Attacks on suspected Bolshevik sympathizers and Jews became commonplace wherever the Whites held sway. Former Mensheviks and SRs were discriminated against to such a degree in White territory that they joined the Bolsheviks en masse where they could and asked their former antagonists to "form a single revolutionary front against the attacks of the counterrevolution and predatory international imperialism."[7] In a sense, Kolchak and Denikin succeeded where so many others had failed in the days before the October Revolution: Together their flawed policies and bad judgment forged an alliance between the Mensheviks and the Bolsheviks, healing a 15-year-old wound in Russian socialism.

THE REDS RESPOND

Struggling to save their revolution and their lives, the Bolsheviks went on the offensive. Near the end of July 1918, Trotsky ordered a draft of all former tsarist junior officers in Soviet Russia; in November, he extended conscription to ex-tsarist field-grade commanders and generals. To ensure the proper motivation for men who had never been remarkably fond of Bolshevism, Trotsky prescribed the death penalty for cowardice or retreat. "Units may and must perish in their entirety but not retreat," an August decree read, "and this must be understood by the commanders and commissars; they must know that there is no turning back."[8] Trotsky added that the families of retreating officers would pay a dear price for disgraceful battlefield conduct; he was, in effect, holding their families hostage.

Harsh disciplinary measures, eerily reminiscent of the imperial army, were instituted among the lower ranks to match

Four Bolshevik leaders, Joseph Stalin, Alexei Rykov, Lev Kamenev, and Gregorii Zinoviev, are photographed on their way to a meeting of the Central Executive Committee of the Communist Party.

those that applied to the officers. Any Red unit charged with cowardice would surrender 10 men at random for execution. Trotsky brought into the twentieth century the ancient practice of decimation. These 10 men would pay for the actions of their comrades regardless of their individual conduct. Anyone doubting Trotsky's resolve was put straight that August, when 20 Red soldiers were shot for their companies' failures in battle.

Trotsky, now commissar of war, also ordered a complete overhaul of the Red Army's structure. Gone were the comradely socialist practices of not saluting or wearing symbols of rank. Formal greeting and shoulder boards were reintroduced. Army groups, known as fronts, were created; divisions were reorganized to increase efficiency. Everywhere, political officers were appointed as the watchdogs of revolutionary consciousness. Field commanders were placed under the watchful gazes of military commissars who regularly reported on the battlefield conduct and political reliability of army officers. A negative evaluation often meant death for any officer unlucky enough to be accused of being insufficiently correct in his thoughts or deeds.

VICTORY

Trotsky's revamped Red Army came into being just as Kolchak and Denikin, who now had complete control over the White armies in the Ukraine, were preparing to move against the Bolsheviks. In January 1919, the Volunteer Army allied itself with several smaller independent anti-Bolshevik formations to become the Armed Forces in the South of Russia. Thus grandiosely renamed, Denikin's army prepared to coordinate with Kolchak in Siberia and with the Allied intervention forces to launch a massive invasion of Soviet Russia.

The resulting 100,000-man offensive began in March and proved to be initially devastating to the Reds. Denikin's and Kolchak's divisions made stunning advances on both fronts. At one point, the Whites moved forward some 360 miles (579.3 kilometers) in just a few weeks, capturing thousands of square miles of territory. The plan they followed was simple: After bursting through the Red defenses, Kolchak and Denikin would link up and wheel around toward Moscow, the new Soviet capital. A separate strike force would move directly on Petrograd. The Whites guaranteed the Western Allies that victory would be gained before the end of the summer, and it seemed in June 1919 that they would make good on their word. Kolchak pushed forward along his entire Siberian front. Denikin smashed one Red division after another, taking the city of Kharkov on June 21 and, nine days later, the river city of Tsaritsyn (the future Stalingrad), where 40,000 Red soldiers became his prisoners.

Lenin and Trotsky, with the Whites bearing down upon them, decided that the best strategy would be to concentrate on bringing down one White front while holding the other in check, to be dealt with in its turn. Kolchak, the weaker of the two enemies, was the first target. Red units massed against him, first halting his offensive and then breaking his lines. By the end of August, a huge gap opened in the center of Kolchak's front, through which the Red Army penetrated beyond the Ural Mountains and deep into Siberia. Over the next two months, Kolchak reeled backward, losing 19,000 men to Bolshevik bullets. Denikin's southern offensive likewise failed. After several attempts to take Moscow

AN AMERICAN REFUSAL

Although the Bolsheviks hoped that their message of working-class fraternity would turn the Allied intervention troops against their mission, sheer exhaustion did the job for them. Most of the Allied troops, especially those among the American contingent, had come to Russia directly from the fighting on the Western Front. Long days and even longer nights patrolling the frozen wastes of northern Russia shattered the men's morale and prompted acts of defiance and protest that many times crossed the line into outright mutiny. The men of one company stationed near the Dvina River went so far as to put their refusal to enter combat into writing:

> To the Commanding Officer of Archangel District; We the under-signed firmly resolve that we demand relief not later than MARCH 15th, 1919
> And after this date we positively refuse to advance on the Bolo [army slang for Bolshevik] lines including patrols and in view of the fact that our object in Russia has been accomplished &

and Petrograd, one of Denikin's field generals, Piotr Wrangel, had to report to headquarters that the fighting had been so costly that his "army has ceased to exist."[9] Meanwhile, morale among the Allied occupation troops dissolved. French soldiers, tired of their Russian adventure and receptive to Bolshevik appeals for working-class solidarity, openly mutinied in some places. Many American and British troops simply refused to fight. All wanted to go home and abandon a seemingly pointless involvement in someone else's civil war.

Their armies and frontlines broken, the Whites were in headlong retreat by December 1919. Just a year earlier, their

having duly acquitted ourselves by doing everything that was in our power to win—and was asked of us, we after 6 months of diligent and uncomplaining sacrifice after serious debate arrive at this conclusion and it is not considered unpatriotic to the U.S. . . . . And whereas [we] find our activity means interference in the affairs of the Russian people with whom we have no quarrel—we do solemnly pledge ourselves to uphold the principles herein stated and to cease all activities on and after above mentioned date.*

The petitioners in this case were neither relieved of duty nor disciplined for their disobedience. One of their commanders simply attributed the refusal to fight as an indication that "regarding the present operations, the men feel that they are contrary to the policy announced when the [American Army] was sent to Russia."**

*Robert L. Willet, **Russian Sideshow: America's Undeclared War, 1918-1920.** Washington, D.C.: Potomac Books, 2003, p. 88.

**Ibid.

leaders and those of the Allied Powers had been confident that Lenin's government and the Bolshevik Revolution could not survive their combined onslaught. Yet Soviet Russia emerged from the fighting intact and firmly under Bolshevik control. "It is impossible to account for the stability of the Bolshevik Government," a British memorandum stated incredulously. "We must admit then that the present Russian government is accepted by the bulk of the Russian people."[10]

The final blows fell in 1920. Admiral Kolchak, attempting to flee Russia with his crumbling army's gold reserve, was captured in January by Red soldiers and summarily shot, his body dumped in a river. Distracted by a brief war with Poland from April to October 1920, the Red Army then resumed its chase of the remnants of Denikin's forces in the late fall. Like Kolchak, Denikin abandoned his men, who then made a frantic attempt to seek shelter with the similarly retreating Allied armies. The Americans, British, French, and Japanese realized that Lenin's party could not be driven from power by force; one by one, they went home, taking as many White refugees as possible with them.

By November 1920, the foreigners were gone, and the counterrevolution had been put down. The Bolshevik regime had been preserved at the cost of 700,000 Red combat casualties and millions of dead or homeless Russian civilians. Soviet power was supreme.

Old Russia Redux

THE FAILED PROMISE OF A NEW DAY

From the party's earliest days, Lenin and the Bolsheviks had promised Russians that a new day was coming within their lifetimes. Karl Marx, however, had theorized that the historical conditions for the transition from capitalism to socialism would take time to develop, and then only after capitalism had reached its fullest development and the end of its usefulness. Lenin had rejected this formulation in its entirety. He claimed that the Bolsheviks actually could craft a socialist state out of a precapitalist social and economic Russia. Indeed, Lenin stood Marxism on its head: First would come the revolution, then the modernization that capitalism was supposed to produce, and finally the transition to socialism and consequently Communism. The Bolshevik Party, according to Lenin, would guide Russia through these stages in its role as the vanguard of the people. Lenin, put simply, planned to take a shortcut on the road to the Communist endpoint Marx had established. It turned out to be a shortcut to disaster.

Instead of being a benevolent proletarian dictatorship that would organize society for the good of the working class, the Soviet Russian government that emerged between the civil war and Lenin's death in January 1924 resembled a fairly typical authoritarian bureaucratic state. In many ways, it was strangely reminiscent of the tsar's government or Kerensky's, with a ruling elite that operated through myriad agencies for its own benefit and was obsessed with maintaining its own political supremacy.

Lenin's promises in virtually every arena went unfulfilled. His attempt to use socialist production methods to sustain Soviet Russia during the civil war, the so-called War Communism, was an utter fiasco that resulted in urban food shortages, rampant inflation, and mass famine among the peasantry. Lenin's "attempt of transition to Communism," as he put it, ended up requiring the Bolsheviks to embrace capitalism anew and seek emergency assistance from, of all places, their old antagonist, the United States.[1] In 1921, Lenin approved an economic revival program known as the New Economic Policy, which allowed for exactly the kind of free-market exchange and profitmaking that the Bolsheviks had sworn to do away with. Similarly, when faced with the prospect of millions of starving Russians, the Bolshevik regime turned to the capitalist United States for aid. As early as July 1921, the United States was furnishing $61 million in food aid to the Soviets. By the following summer, the American Relief Administration (ARA) was feeding more than 11 million Russians every day. The goodwill generated by the ARA prompted the Russian author Maxim Gorky to say of the U.S. effort that it was "a unique, gigantic achievement, worthy of the greatest glory, which will long remain in the memory of millions of Russians . . . whom you have saved from death."[2] Gorky thanked the United States, not the Bolsheviks; capitalism had succeeded where War Communism had failed. Lenin's new day had not dawned.

FROM REVOLUTION TO DICTATORSHIP

After Lenin's government had to beg for help from one of the world's preeminent capitalist powers, Bolshevik economic promises faded completely into a dull haze of shared hardship. Russians were supposed to partake equally in the benefits of socialist modernization; everyone would live a life of comfort and abundance. Instead, Russians suffered together through repeated crop failures, bungled food distribution schemes, and industrial mismanagement. The Bolsheviks neither produced the material benefits they had trumpeted, nor did they bring the liberty Russians had been traditionally denied. The freedom Lenin had spoken of became meaningless before it even had been realized. Lenin's socialist state became characterized by constant surveillance and arbitrary arrests. Political critics were rounded up, given show trials, and imprisoned in one of the 315 special camps that eventually were established to hold opponents of the regime. Workers and soldiers who complained of Bolshevik excesses were ordered to be silent. An uprising of disillusioned Kronstadt sailors in 1921 was put down through the use of raw armed force. Bolshevik freedom was transformed into tyranny.

"The Bolsheviks," wrote the scholar Robert Service, by 1924 "had an unshakable monopoly of power."[3] Yet the party's promises of social equality, economic justice, and political liberty for the oppressed masses had evaporated. The socialist slogans about a protetariat state remained, but the dream of a Communist future had disappeared. All that was left was empty propaganda and business as usual in Russia.

There would be no transition to a better world while Lenin was alive, and certainly not after he died in 1924, following a series of strokes. Preparing Russia for the days ahead without him, Lenin had warned the party to beware of one man, Joseph Stalin. Already suffering in 1922 from impaired judgment, Lenin passed over Trotsky for the role of party general secretary. It was a decision he and Russia would soon regret. The person Lenin supported at the time as party leader was Stalin. Yet by late 1923, almost totally incapacitated and obviously dying, Lenin rightly feared that "Comrade Stalin, having become General Secretary, has concentrated limitless power in his hands, and I am not certain that he will always be careful enough in his use of this power."[4] He went on to warn the party against allowing Stalin any more power. Lenin's old friend Bukharin sensed even better the danger posed by Stalin. "Stalin will strangle us," he warned his comrades. "He is an unprincipled intriguer who subordinates everything to his lust for power."[5] Trotsky similarly sounded alarm bells over Stalin's ascension to party control.

Stalin's response to all this was to wait out Lenin's death. After having Lenin's body embalmed and entombed in a manner that recalled the treatment of saints in the Orthodox Church, Stalin moved against anyone who stood between him and ultimate rule. Opponents were all purged from the party and executed. Trotsky, living in exile in Mexico since being expelled from the Communist Party after Lenin died, was assassinated in 1940 on Stalin's orders. Freed from both Lenin's memory and the threat of his old associates, Stalin proceeded to create his own personal empire out of the remnants of the Bolshevik Revolution. Between 1924 and 1937, he assembled a totalitarian machine operated exclusively by himself. The Communist Party of the Soviet Union became an extension of his will, his megalomania, and his paranoia. Stalin scoffed at the worldwide socialist revolution that Bolshevism had proposed, and he replaced it with the dubious notion of Socialism in One Country, as he labeled it. Stalin's Russia would isolate itself and move into the future in the direction and at the pace that Stalin chose.

Pictured, an official celebration honoring Joseph Stalin on his birthday. After Stalin's death in 1953, efforts made by Stalin's successor, Nikita Khrushchev, helped to dismantle the cult of personality Stalin had created for himself in the Soviet Union.

In order to make sure that the transformation from the Bolshevik Revolution to a Stalinist dictatorship was completed and secured, Stalin turned to Felix Dzerzhinsky's, and later Lavrenty Beria's, secret police. Using a ruthless state organization that became the NKVD and later evolved into the Cold War KGB, Stalin swept millions of Russians into prisons and labor camps, from which many never returned. Only the German dictator Adolf Hitler established a camp system to rival the Soviet *gulags* in their inhumane cruelty and total disregard for human dignity and justice.

In the early 1930s, Stalin compounded the political terror he was creating with a program of forced industrialization and farm collectivization that cost an estimated 10 million Russians their lives. Later in the decade, in a further attempt to remake

Russia in his own image, Stalin cleared the Red Army of officers who even hinted at having their own political or military views, thus substantially weakening the Russian defenses at a time when Nazi Germany was growing vastly stronger. When the German armies invaded Russia in June 1941, untold numbers of Soviet soldiers paid in blood for Stalin's vanity and paranoid delusions. The courage and devotion of those who remained was enough to win the Second World War and allow Stalin to claim the credit.

THE RETURN OF THE TSARS

At the time of Stalin's death in 1953, the Soviet Union bore no resemblance to the proletarian paradise Lenin had sketched out for the Russian people. The Soviet Union of the 1950s through the 1980s was a police-state dictatorship that developed into a global military superpower. Throughout the second half of the twentieth century, Russia embarked on a program of overseas expansion, international intrigue, and military adventurism that could only be described as blatantly imperialistic. Western scholars and politicians accurately portrayed the Soviet Union as an empire, complete with enormous military forces and the nuclear capacity to annihilate its rivals; economists noted that Russia possessed a class system and routinely engaged in market exchanges that were every bit as capitalistic as those of non-socialist countries. Bolshevik values and principles by then existed only in the pages of Russian history books.

Soviet Russia, by the last decade of the twentieth century, looked nothing like the proletarian state envisaged by Lenin more than 70 years earlier. The USSR had drifted widely and irreversibly from its socialist path. Its society, culture, and worldview, in the words of historian John Gooding, did not "point towards a communist fulfillment, and if anything pointed *away* from it."[6] Politically spent, ideologically empty, and materially broken, Soviet Russia disintegrated in December 1991, when the Communist Party simply voted its regime out

Vladimir Putin lights a candle on the seventieth anniversary of Stalin's Great Purge of 1937–1938. After serving two terms as president (1999–2008), Putin became Russia's prime minister in 2008. Some independent Russian media outlets and many Western commentators have criticized several actions made during his presidency as being antidemocratic.

of power. Notwithstanding a coup attempt by diehard military officers, the Soviet Union disappeared. The Bolshevik experiment, begun with such energy, ended in complete exhaustion, and the Russian people started over.

Confused, disappointed, and dispirited, Russians cast about for a successor to Bolshevism in which they could have some measure of faith. Traditional Russian autocracy filled that need.

VLADIMIR PUTIN

Vladimir Putin was born in Leningrad (now St. Petersburg) on October 7, 1952, within weeks of the thirty-fifth anniversary of the Bolshevik Revolution. The only child of a factory worker, Putin grew up in a crowded communal apartment where the struggle for place and recognition was paramount. As a boy, he studied judo while attending the rather exclusive Leningrad School 281. Putin's sharp mind and scholarly habits led him to Leningrad University and law school in 1970. His university class load, however, did not stop the strapping young Putin from becoming the city's judo champion in 1975. After graduation, Putin joined the KGB, the Soviet security service, then moved to Moscow and underwent intense training in espionage and foreign languages, specializing in German. Putin later was assigned to a KGB post in the former East Germany, where he spied on NATO military operations and recruited new secret agents. He returned to Russia after Communism's fall in 1991 and served in several political posts, including that of head of the new Russian security service, the FSB, until he was appointed president of the Russian Federation in December 1999. In March 2008, Putin gave up his presidency to Dmitri Medvedev and accepted the office of prime minister, from which he continues to assert an overwhelming influence on Russian domestic and foreign affairs.

Although cloaked in the trappings of democracy, the system that replaced Bolshevism/Communism looked very much like the tsarist one that Lenin thought he had demolished. Under President Boris Yeltsin (1991–1999) and even more so under his successor, Vladimir Putin (1999–2008), Russians stepped back into a half-forgotten world of maturing capitalism, guided by an authoritarian state and led by a single man. Putin especially gave back to ordinary Russians their dreams of a stable, secure, and prosperous future.

The new Russia, under Putin, would look forward into the twenty-first century as the old one had gazed ahead into the twentieth century—with an abiding hope that the decades to come would be better than the ones that had passed. Russians had turned back time to find what the Bolsheviks had failed to provide. Perhaps it is between the covers of the textbooks Russian schoolchildren learn from that one finds the most succinct expression of the new tsarism. They speak of a Russia boldly moving forward under the care of a leader who symbolizes everything the nation is and strives to become. As one textbook states, "Now everyone says: 'Russia, Putin, Unity!'"[7] The Bolsheviks and the Communists after them had unwittingly served as the caretakers for the old Russia. Their legacy is ironically one of preservation rather than creation. The new day, it seems, will have to wait.

CHRONOLOGY

1870   **April**   Vladimir Ulyanov (Lenin) is born.

1894   **November**   Nicholas II becomes the tsar.

1905   **January**   Bloody Sunday demonstrations end in a massacre.

        October   Nicholas II issues the October Manifesto.

1914   **August**   Russia enters the First World War.

1917   **February**   Provisional Government formed in response to civil disorder; Kerensky soon appointed as minister of justice; Tsar Nicholas II abdicates.

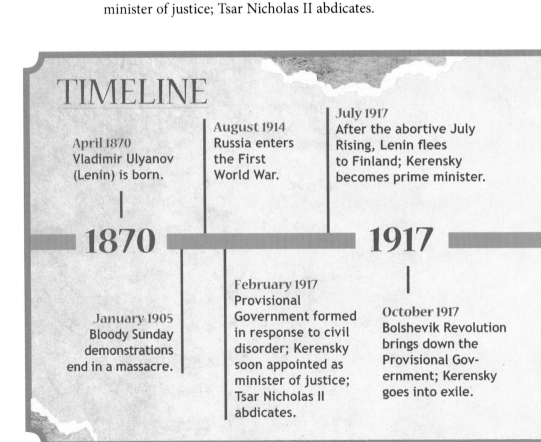

TIMELINE

April 1870
Vladimir Ulyanov
(Lenin) is born.

August 1914
Russia enters
the First
World War.

July 1917
After the abortive July
Rising, Lenin flees
to Finland; Kerensky
becomes prime minister.

1870

1917

January 1905
Bloody Sunday
demonstrations
end in a massacre.

February 1917
Provisional
Government formed
in response to civil
disorder; Kerensky
soon appointed as
minister of justice;
Tsar Nicholas II
abdicates.

October 1917
Bolshevik Revolution
brings down the
Provisional Gov-
ernment; Kerensky
goes into exile.

1917   **March** Grand Duke Michael refuses the crown.

April Lenin returns to Petrograd.

July After the abortive July Rising, Lenin flees to Finland; Kerensky becomes prime minister.

August Kornilov's revolt occurs; Bolsheviks form the Red Guards.

September Bolsheviks gain control of Petrograd Soviet; Lenin returns to Russia in disguise.

October Bolshevik Revolution brings down the Provisional Government; Kerensky goes into exile.

1918   **January** Red Army is formed in response to White counterrevolutionaries gathering in the Ukraine and Siberia.

January 1918
Red Army is formed in response to White counter-revolutionaries gathering in the Ukraine and Siberia.

August 1919
Red Army counterattacks against Kolchak and Denikin; both White armies in retreat by December and are defeated by early 1920.

1918

1924

March 1918
Bolshevik Party is officially renamed the Communist Party of Russia; Treaty of Brest-Litovsk concluded.

January 1924
Lenin dies.

1918   **April** Japanese forces land at Vladivostok, beginning the foreign intervention.

          March Bolshevik Party is officially renamed the Communist Party of Russia; Treaty of Brest-Litovsk is concluded.

          May Czech Legion openly rebels against Bolshevik regime.

          June British troops land at Murmansk; French join them two months later.

          July The Romanovs are executed.

          September Americans intervene in the civil war, landing at Archangel and Vladivostok.

1919   **March** White offensive begins, aimed at destroying Bolshevik power.

          August Red Army counterattacks against Kolchak and Denikin; both White armies in retreat by December and are defeated by early 1920.

1920   **April** Russia wars with Poland.

          November The last of the foreign intervention troops leave Russia.

1924   **January** Lenin dies.